BOSCH

BOSCH

Reality, symbol and fantasy

Isidro Bango Torviso / Fernando Marías

Silex

© SILEX®: 1982
I.S.B.N.: 84-85041-60-7
Depósito legal: VI. 212 - 1982
Copyright:
Layout: J. M. Dominguez
Printed in Spain by H. Fournier, S.A. - Vitoria
(Printed in Spain)
Translated by:
Josephine Breggazzi

To Illiana, Clara, Isabel and Teresa

CONTENTS

I
REALITY
AND IMAGINATION

«There are also some works with diverse extravagances, in which seas, skies, woods, fields and many other things are disfigured, some coming out of a sea clam, others defecated by herons, women and men, with black and white people in diverse acts and attitudes, birds, animals of all types and of great naturalness, such pleasant and fantastic things that they could not by any means be described to anyone who had no knowledge of them.»

It might cause us no small surprise to learn that the above lines come from the first description and judgement on the *Garden of Delights* of which we have any knowledge (1), in which the impressions of the Italian, Antonio de Beatis —written in 1517— just a year after Bosch's death, when the companion of Cardenal Luis de Aragón visited the collection of paintings which Henry III of Nassau owned in his Brussels palace. The phrases which Antonio de Beatis dedicated to the painting in the Prado Museum may sound strange to our ears for we currently view Bosch's works with quite different eyes to those of this Italian of the *Cinquecento*. Our interest in the paintings of the master of Hertogenbosch is centred on other, quite different aspects to those which moved Antonio de Beatis to express himself thus. Yet he was not the only one of this time who thus regarded Bosch's works —could we not also speak at the same time of Bosch himself?

M.A. Michiel, in his «Notizie d'opere di disegno», written a few years later (2), judged three of Bosch's works which belonged to the Venetian collection on of Cardenal Grimaldi (among them the *Visions of the Hereafter* of the Ducal Palace in Venice and a now disappeared *Jonah*), and

---

(1) Quoted by Ernst H. Gombrich. «The earliest Description of Bosch's Garden of Delight». *Journal of the Warburg and Courtauld Institutes,* 1967 p. 403-6.

(2) M. A. Michiel. *Notizie d'opere di disegno* (1521-1543). Michiel visited the works Cardenal Grimani possessed in Venice in 1521, among which were the *Vision of the Hereafter* from the Ducal Palace in Venice and a panel of *Jonah and the Whale* which is today missing.

pointed out that despite having been one of the first painters to work with oils (3), Bosch had managed to achieve a much gentler register (*morbido*) than that of other artists who had used this technique.

Felipe de Guevara himself (4), the gentleman-in-waiting of Charles V and a traveller to Flanders, the great collector of Bosch's works, inherited from his father Don Diego in 1520 which seven years after his death were to be bought from his heirs by Philip II (1570), and the author of one of the first Spanish books on artistic matters, the «Comentarios de la pintura» (*Comments on painting*), wrote around 1560:

> «There was in olden times another genre of painting which was called *Grillo*. *Antiphilus* gave it this name while he was painting a man, whom in pleasaunce he called *Grillo*. From thence it was that this genre of painting be called *Grillo*. Antiphilus was born in Egypt and learned this genre of painting from Ctesidenus, which to my judgement was similar to that which our generation praises in Hieronymus Bosch or Bosco as we say, who always exerted himself to discover details of odd men and of rare postures to paint...» (5).

In this first passage, Don Felipe with the mind of a Renaissance antiquarian, relates Bosch's works to the old type of painting called «grillos» (crickets»), a genre recorded by Pliny in his «Natural History». In the first place, he interprets Bosch's oddities in a eupheuistic way, alleging precedents in classical Antiquity. He might even have related them to the Roman and Renaissance «grotesques» the fantasies and monstrosities of which provided a polemical subject for scholars of ancient and contemporary art. One should bear in mind that the grotesques, despite the success they enjoyed in Imperial Rome and during the Renaissance, were repeatedly condemned by Vitruvius and a large number of treatise-writers of the *Quattrocento* on the grounds that they did not stick to natu-

---

(3) An obvious mistake for, within the Flemish artistic environment oil painting was carried out from the beginning of the 15th century. The general idea of the times, more mythical than real, was that Jan van Eyck was the inventor of this new technique.

(4) See Francisco Javier Sánchez Cantón. *Fuentes literarias para la Historia del Arte español.* Madrid, 1923. I, p. 159 ff. Originally in Felipe de Guevara *Comentarios de la pintura,* ed. Antonio Ponz., Madrid, 1788, p. 41 ff.

(5) The painting of «grillos» (*gryllos* in Greek means pig), according to Pliny, was a genre made fashionable by the Greco-Egyptian Antiphilus round about 300 B. C., who portrayed one such «Grillo» or so-called for its swinish aspect. This term was used from Antiquity to denote scenes with semi-human and semi-animal figures. «Grillo» was also the name of one of Ulysses' companions who, according to Homer's Odissy, was metamorphosed by Circe into an animal. Human figures in which several parts of the body have been eliminated are also called «grillos» such as the trunk, thus reducing its form to a head and pair of legs.

ral reality but were fantastic representations of «things which neither are nor can be», as Guevara himself stated, in another passage of his book on painting. Another estimate was to oppose this negative one around the middle of the 16th. century, and was representative of contemporary artistic mannerism which exalted the virtues of the grotesque as a field of activity for the personal fantasy of the artist. Towards the end of the century, mainly with Pirro Ligorio and Giampaolo Lomazzo, art theorists tried a new means of justification for such extravagances, pointing out the symbolic nature of the grotesques (of the ancients almost as if they were hieroglyphics, but not of the moderns). With this change of attitude, what was impossible in nature was justified as «possible» as the result of logical activity based on a world of symbolic and esoteric symbols (6). However, Lomazzo himself, for whom the grotesques and other fantastic chimeras were mysterious symbols, was to write in this «Trattato dell'arte della pittura» (1584) on Bosch, without at any point referring to the symbolic nature of his works to assert that he had been unique and *veramente divino* in his representations of horrifying things and strange apparitions or dreadful nightmares (7).

Felipe de Guevara in turn rejects the accusation which then hung over the painter of Hertogenbosch for painting meaningless fantasies, «without discretion or judgement whatsoever», and defends his «naturalism» by analysing his solutions and justifying their use:

«And thus Hieronymus Bosch has come before us, it would be only right to correct the vulgar, and others more than vulgar, of an error they have conceived of his paintings, and that is that any monstrosity or thing outside nature that they see they straightway attribute to Hieronymus Bosch, making him the inventor of monsters and chimeras. I do not deny that he paints strange ephigies of things, but this was only to the end of painting Hell in which matter, wishing to portray devils, he imagined compositions of wonderful things.

This which Hieronymus Bosch did with prudence and decorum, others do without discretion or judgement whatsoever. For, having witnessed how well accepted in Flanders that genre of painting of Hieronymus Bosch was, they agreed to imitate him, painting monsters and delirious imaginings, giving out that the imitation of Bosch consisted only in this. Thus the paintings of this

(6) On grotesques in general and criticism of same from Vitruvius, see Nicole Dacos. *La découverte de la Domus Aurea et la formation des grotesques à la Renaissance.* Londres-Leide, 1969. p. 121-35 and Appendix II (with the text by Pirro Ligorio on grotesques).

(7) Giampaolo Lomazzo. *Trattato dell'arte della pittura, scultura ed architettura.* Milan, 1584.

genre are infinite, stamped with the name of Hieronymus Bosch falsely ins-
cribed, on which it never crossed his mind to lay his hands; what is laid there
is smoke and little wit, smoking them at the chimney-place to give them au-
thority and antiquity.

One thing I dare assert about Bosch, who never painted anything unnatural
in his life if it were not the matter of Hell or Purgatory, as I have said. His inventions were based on seeking the rarest but natural things, in such a way
that it could be a universal law that any painting, although signed by Bosch,
in which there were any monstrosity or thing which surpasses the limits of
nature that is adulterated and feigned, if it is not, as I say, that the painting is about Hell, or any matter concerned with it.

It is true, and it will be evident to anyone who observes Bosch's works dili-
gently, that he strictly observes decorum and keeps carefully within the limits of Nature, just as much or more as any other artist. But it is only fair to
point out that among these imitators of Hieronymus Bosch there is one who
was his disciple who out of devotion to his master or else to give credit to
his works, wrote the name Bosch on his paintings instead of his own. Despite this, his are paintings to be admired and he who possesses them should
hold them in high esteem, for in their inventions and moralities, he followed
his master's steps and was more patient and diligent than Bosch in his work,
without departing from his master's grace and elegance and colouring. An
example of this type of painting is a table which V.M. has on which the seven
deadly sins are painted in a circle, displayed in figures and examples, and
although the whole painting is in itself wonderful, the portrait of Envy to my
mind is so rare and ingenious, and so well expressed to give the right effect,
that it could compete with Aristedes, the inventor of these paintings which
the Greeks called Ethice, which in our Castilian sounds the same as Paintings which show the customs and affections of men's souls.»

We once more find here Renaissance preoccupation and interest for
the formal aspect and the propriety of Bosch's works: «he strictly observes decorum and keeps carefully within the limits of Nature», works with
«grace and elegance» and beautiful «colouring» —and not a single word
about the problems of significance which are today perhaps the greatest
attraction of Bosch's paintings. However, we have here a clear attempt
at classification of some of his works— or parts of them. Felipe de Guevara compares the scene in «Envy» to the table of the *Seven Deadly Sins*
(now in the Prado Museum) (8) with the paintings of Aristedes, their my-

---

(8) Despite Felipe de Guevara's attribution of the Table of the *Seven Deadly Sins* to an anonymous
disciple of Bosch's, critics coincide almost unanimously in assigning it as one of the works of
the master of Hertogenbosch.

thical inventor, and includes them in the genre of «ethical» works, or works which show «the customs and affections of men's souls». That means paintings of manners and as a final corollary, moral and didactic ones.

In another context, in a letter sent to Philip II in 1563, Guevara's commentaries on Bosch are of a somewhat different tone, although they abound in certain aspects already mentioned in the former one. The collector of Bosch's works reiterates the fact that Bosch had never painted anything outside the limits of Nature that had no relation to the underworld or to Purgatory. He adds that Bosch's inventions were based on the investigation of extremely rare but always natural things, and ends by repeating his argument on the limitations of the Fleming's paintings. On the one hand, we are faced with practical advice with a view to the correct identification of Bosch's works, differentiating them from false apocryphal imitations. On the other hand, Guevara attemps a full explanation of the procedures followed by the painter to create his «fantasies»: Bosch uses very strange objects, but always natural ones, to portray visions of unnatural, invisible or irreal objects from the phenomenic point of view, although they exist in the supernatural reality of Hell, a reality based on then prevailing, deeply-rooted religious Christian beliefs if we are to consider this reality as such.

Despite these demarcations of Guevara's, one should turn to another contemporary author, Ambrosio de Morales, to discover in his humanistically accurate and univeral vision, something which spiritually reflects the anxiety that Bosch's works arouse in us today. Contrary to Antonio de Beatis, Michiel or Guevara himself, Morales –the author of the erudite «Antiquities of the Cities of Spain» (1575)– is concerned with giving us what for him was the key to the meaning of *The Haycart* (today in the Prado Museum in Madrid). Thus, he reminds us of the Flemish proverb in which Bosch must have found inspiration and which gives meaning to his triptych. In «Cebes' Table», in the third part of his «Moral Theatre», written before 1546 but published in 1586, he tells us in his description of the painting (9): «... and it must be understood as a haycart, in Flemish, which is tantamount to a cart of trifles in Castilian». Men chase after the cart, try to climb up onto it, even kill themselves for this cartful of futilities, of mundane passing fancies and perishable *vanitas*.

---

(9) Ambrosio de Morales. *Ceres'Panel* in *The Moral Theatre*. Madrid, 1586; quoted by A. M. Salazar in «El Bosco y Ambrosio de Morales». *Archivo Español de Arte*. 1955, p. 117 ff.

THE HAYCART *(frag.).* Prado Museum, Madrid.

Something similar occurs in the «History of the Order of Saint Jerome» (1605) by Fray José de Sigüenza, who, on account of the moral and religious preoccupations typical of his time and environment –and his own, too, for which we should need to come back to this subject– wrote in 1599 (10):

«... that I wish to speak at more length for certain reasons: for his great ingenuity deserves it, for they are commonly called the follies of Hieronymus Bosch by people who little stop to think on what they look at, and because I think that he is unjustly slandered as a heretic. I have such a concept (to begin at the end) of the piety and zeal of the King, our founder (Philip II), that if I knew this to be so, I would not allow the paintings within his house, within his cloisters, within his chamber, within the chapters and vestry. All these places are adorned with them. Without this reason, which for me is great, there is another to be taken from his paintings: almost all the Sacraments and states and degrees of the Church are to be seen in them, from the Pope to the lowest, two points on which heretics stumble, and he painted them from many angles and with great consideration, which he would not have done had he been a heretic, as likewise he did the same with the mysteries of our Redemption. I wish to show now that his paintings are not follies, but books of great prudence and artifice, and if they are follies, then the follies are ours and not his, and to state once and for all that his works are painted satires of men's sins and effronteries...»

«... the difference which there is to my mind between this man's paintings and those of others, is that the others try to paint Man as he appears on the outside: this man only dared to paint him as he is within. To this end he worked with a singular motive which I shall state with this example: poets and painters are very close in the opinion of all (11); the closely germane faculties which are no further removed than the brush from the pen, which are almost one and the same; the subjects, the ends, the colours, the licences and other parts are so similar that they can hardly be distinguished lest it be by the formalities of our metaphysics. Among the Latin poets there is one (and not any other who deserves a name) who, although he might resemble him, could not equal Virgil's heroic quality, nor the comic or tragic quality of Terence or Seneca, nor Horace's lyrical strain, and although he might be more excellent and his spirit promise much, these would have to come first, he decided to take another path: he invented a ridiculous type of poetry which he

(10) Fray José de Sigüenza. *Historia de la Orden de San Gerónimo.* II Part, Madrid 1600. III, Book IV, discourse XVIII.
(11) An opinion based on the idea of painting as the literature for the illiterate upheld at least since Horace's maxim of *ut pictura poesis* and generally in force in the 16th century in the theoretic artistic literature of the time. On this subject, see Rensselaer W. Lee's article: «*Ut pictura poesis.* The humanist theory of Painting». *The Art Bulletin,* XXII, 1940. p. 195-268.

called macarronic. Being like this, as he had such a talent, such inventive powers and such ingenuity, he was ever prince and chief of this style, and thus all good wits read higit ommia. And because his state and profession did not seem to allow this sort of occupation (he was a clergyman and I shall not tell his name for he kept it secret) he made up a ridiculous name and called himself Merlin Cocayo, which fits in well with the surface of the work, as does that of the other writer called Aesop. In his poems he reveals with singular artifice how much good one may desire and take from the most prized poets, both in moral matters as in those of Nature, and if I had to perform the work of critic here, I would show the truth of this with the collation and counterpoint of many examples. It was this poet, I am certain, that Hieronymus Bosch wished to resemble, not because he had seen him, for I believe that he painted before this other one ever scribbled, but because he was moved by the same thought and motive, he knew he had a great natural talent for painting and that however much he did, Albert Dürer, Michelangelo, Urbino and others would always be ahead of him; he opened up a new path so that others went after him and he after none, and drew the eyes of all to himself; a sort of painting like a joke, macarronic which threw among all those mockeries many fine strange things, both in their invention and in their execution and painting, at times revealing how much he was worth in that art, as did likewise Cocayo, if truth be said.»

After these explanations of Bosch's religious orthodoxy, his motivations for opening up new «macarronic» paths, the art of painting and the piously didactic finality of his works, the Castilian Hieronymite goes on to analyse the works preserved in the Philippine monastry of San Lorenzo del Escorial, dividing them in three types. The first of these is that of scenes from the Life of Christ:

«The tableaux and pictures herein are three different types. Either he paints devout subjects, as are the stages of the Life of Chirst and His Passion, the Adoration of the Magi and when He is carrying the Cross: in the first, he expresses the pious and sincere affection of the wise and virtous, in which there is no monstrosity nor folly to be seen; in the other he displays the envy and wrath of false wisdom, which does not rest until it has taken the life of the innocent, who is Christ. Thus the Pharisees and Scribes are to be seen with furious faces, fierce, scowling figures in whose habits and actions may be read the fury of these feelings.»

In the second place, the subject of the temptations of Saint Anthony:

«He painted the temptations of Saint Anthony one by one (which is the second type of painting) as this was a subject in which he could achieve strange effects.

On the one hand this Saint, the Prince of Hermits, may be seen with a serene, devout, contemplative face, his soul at ease and full of peace; on the other, there are the infinite fantasies and monsters shaped by the Foe to harrow, disconcert and perturb that pious soul and steadfast love; to this end, he depicts animals, wild beasts, chimeras, monsters, fires, deaths, screams, threats, vipers, lions, dragons and dreadful birds of so many kinds that it is wonderous how he could have conceived so many ideas. And all this to show that a soul helped by Divine Grace, and taken by its hand to such a way of life, although in fantasy and from without and within the Foe seems to move one to laughter or vain delight, or wrath and other disorderly passions, this would not be sufficient to overthrow him nor to budge him from his purpose. He varied this subject and thought so many times and with so many new inventions that I wonder how he could find so much and I stop to consider my own poverty and weakness and how far I am from that perfection, for with such easy trivialities and trifles I become perturbed and disconcerted, I lose my cell, silence, withdrawal, and even patience, and in this Saint's case, all the devil's and Hell's cunning to overcome him could avail so little; and the Lord is just as ready to succour me as him, if I join the fight courageously.»

Later on, after describing the Table of the *Seven Deadly Sins,* Sigüenza discusses the third type of works «not of lesser worth, although they appear more macarronic», and enters into the description of the *Haycart* and *The Garden of Delights,* which is so vivid and well written that we cannot resist the temptation of quoting a long passage from it:

«... in His Majesty's chamber, where he has a case of books like that of the clergy, there is an excellent panel and picture: Our Redeemer is placed in the middle as if in the centre of it within a circumference of light and glory; on its contour, there are seven other circles in which the Seven Deadly Sins may be seen, with which all creatures whom He redeemed offend Him without thinking that He is watching them and sees all. In another seven rings (12), he afterwards put the seven Sacraments with which He enriched His Church, and where, as in precious vessels he placed the remedy for so many faults and sufferings in which men let themselves fall, which is surely the thought of a pious man and good for us to see ourselves therein, for he painted it like mirrors in which Christianity is reflected; whoever painted this could not feel ill against our Faith. Therein may be seen the Pope, the Bis-

---

(12) A panel mentioned by Father Sigüenza as existing in the Escorial monastery at the end of the 16th century and now missing. It would naturally go with the Table of the *Seven Deadly Sins,* although maybe seven oppositive virtues would have been more suitable —although more difficult to portray in anecdotic form: meekness, humbleness, chastity, temperance, diligence, etc.

hops and Priests, some taking orders, others baptising, others confessing and administering the sacraments. Without these pictures, there are others of great ingenuity and no less worth, although they seem more macarronic, which is the third type of his inventions.

The thought and artifice of them is based on that passage from Isaiah (Isaiah 41) in which at God's command he shouts aloud: «All flesh is as hay and all its glory as the flowers of the field»; and on what David says (Psalm 103): «As for man, his days are as grass: as a flower of the field, so he flourisheth». One of these pictures has the first as its basis or main subject, which is the cart loaded with hay upon which are seated the delights of the flesh, fame and the display of their glory and power figured in some naked women playing and singing, and fame in the figure of the devil near them with his wings and trumpet which announces his greatness and gifts. The other has as its basis and main theme a flowerlet and little fruit of the kind we call strawberries, which are like madronas and which are called in some parts «maiotas», a fruit which is no sooner tasted than it is finished. In order that its argument may be understood, I shall expound it in the order in which it is disposed. Between both side tableaux, there is a large picture and two doors which shut together. On the first of these doors, the Creation of Man is painted, and as God sets him in Paradise and in a pleasant place full of green and delightful foliage, the Lord of all the animals of the earth and of the birds of the air, and as He commands him to exercise obedience and faith unto Him, thus must he not eat of one tree; and after, as the Devil tricks him in the guise of a serpent, he eats and trespasses God's precept and He expels him from that delectable place and from that state of high dignity in which he had been created and placed. In the picture called Haycart this is painted more simply; in the one of the strawberry-tree it is done with a thousand fantasies and imaginings which have much to teach us; this is in the first part and on the door. In the large picture which follows, man occupies this painting, expelled from Paradise and thrust into this world; and he declares that it is to seek a glory of hay, straw or grass without fruit, which is today and which tomorrow is put in the oven, as God Himself says; and thus he reveals the lives, the exercises and speeches with which these children of sin and wrath, forgetful of God's command which is to atone for their sins and raise up the eyes of faith to a Saviour who is to redeem them, turn to seek and try out the glory of the flesh, which is as brief hay, finite useless, for such are the gifts of sensuality, states, ambition and fame. This haycart in which this glory journeys is drawn by seven wild beasts, brutes and dreadful monsters, in which creaturs half-man and half-lion are painted, others half-dogs, others half-bears, half-fishes, half-wloves, all symbols and figures of Pride, Lasciviousness, Avarice, Ambition, Bestiality, Tyranny, Sagacity and Brutality. Around this cart all estates of man are placed, from the Pope and Emperor and other Princes, to those who have the lowest estate and humblest trades of the earth, for all flesh is as grass and the children of

24

TABLE OF THE SEVEN DEADLY SINS. Prado Museum, Madrid.

the flesh will twist and use all to achieve that vain, fleeting glory; and all this is but to give clues as to how to climb up to the glory of this cart: some prop ladders against it, others use hooks, others creep up, others jump and seek whatever means and instruments they may to get up there; some who were already up on the top fall down below, others are caught up in the wheels, others delight in that vain name and air. Thus there is no estate, nor exercise, nor trade, be it high or low, human or divine which the sons of this century do not turn or abuse of to attain and enjoy this glory of hay. I know full well that all walk on in haste, and the animals which pull the cart strain because it is heavily laden, and they tug at it to end their day's work quickly, to unload that journey's burden and return for another, which only too well displays the brevity of this wretched century and the little time it takes to pass, and how alike are all times in malice. The end and destination of all this is painted on the back door, on which an appalling hell may be seen, with strange torments, dreadful monsters, all shrouded in darkness and eternal fire. And to give an idea of the crowd of those that enter therein but do not fit therein, he depicts how new chambers and quarters are being built, and the stones which rise upwards to erect the building are the souls of the wretched damned, there turned also into instruments of their torment by the same means which they used to attain that glory. And so that it may also be understood that divine Piety and Succour never totally forsake even the greatest sinners, even though they be in the midst of their sins, the Guardian Angel is to be seen next to him who is on top of the haycart in the midst of his ungainly vices, praying to God for him, and the Lord Jesus Christ with open arms and the stigmata made manifest, awaiting those that repent.»

«I confess that I read more things in this panel, in one brief glance, than in other books in many days. The other panel of vain glory and brief happiness of the strawberry-tree, and its hardly perceptible aroma, smelled when it is past, is the most ingenious thing and the greatest artifice which could be imagined. I tell the truth when I say that if it was taken as a purpose and if some great wit should wish to proclaim it, he would make a very profitable book of it, for in it may be seen as though alive and clear, infinite places of the Scriptures which touch upon man's malice, for how many allegories or metaphors there are in them to mean this, in the Prophets and in the Psalms, beneath tame, brave, fierce, lazy sagacious, cruel, meat-eating animals, beasts of burden or work, for pleasure and leasure or show, sought in men and turned into beasts through their inclinations and habits. And the mixture made of one and another, all are depicted here with admirable propriety. The same may be said for the birds and the fishes and reptiles, for Divine Writing is full of them all. Here also may be understood that transmigration of souls which Pythagoras, Plato and other poets described, who made learned fables of these metamorphoses and transformations, who attempted no more than show us bad habits, customs or sinister warnings in which the souls

TABLE OF THE SEVEN DEADLY SINS. *Sloth.* Prado Museum, Madrid.

of wretched men are arrayed, who are lions in pride, tigers in vengeance, mules in lasciviousness or horses or swine, fish in tyranny, peacocks in vainglory, foxes in sagacity and diabolic ruses, monkeys and wolves in gluttony, asses in senselessness and malice, she-asses in simplicity sheep, kids in mischievousness and other such accidents and forms which impose and build on this human being. And thus these monsters and oddities are made and all for such a vile and lowly end as is the taste for vengeance, for sensuality, for a concern for reputation, for appearance and esteem, and other such things which hardly come to one's palate, let alone wet one's mouth, such as the taste and flavour of a strawberry and the perfume of its flowers, for many even sustain themselves with its perfume.

I should like everybody to be as full of the transfers of this picture as they are of the truth and the original whence Hieronymus Bosch portrayed his oddities, for apart from the great skill, the ingenuity, the strangeness and imaginings which there are in every thing (it is wonderous how one sole head could have come across so many) great profit would be drawn thereof if each saw in it his own living portrait from within, unless he does not notice what is within himself and is so blind that he cannot recognise the passions and vices which so disfigure him in a beast or in so many beasts. And he would also see in the last tableau the wretched end and destination of his studies, exercises and ocupations, and that they turn into those infernal dwelling-places. He who put all his happiness in music and vain, lascivious songs, in dances, in games, in hunts, in fine clothes, in riches, in orders, in vengeance, in the esteem of holiness and hypocrisy, will see a counterpoint in the same genre, and that brief flavour will be turned into eternal wrath, irremediable and implacable. I do not wish to say more of Hieronymus Bosch's oddities. I would only say that in almost all his paintings, I mean in those which possess this wit (for as we have seen there are other simple, holy ones), he puts fire and an owl. With the first of these he gives us to understand that one should be mindful of that eternal fire, that in this way any work will become easy, as is to be seen in all the panels he painted of Saint Anthony. And by the second of these he means that his paintings are the fruit of care and study and must be observed with study. The owl is a nocturnal bird, devoted to Minerva and to study, a symbol of the Athenians where Philsophy so flourished which is attained with the quiet and silence of the night, by spending more oil than wine.»

In Fray José de Sigüenza are fused an esteem for Bosch's art on formal grounds and, even more so, an admiration for his painting of a moral, edifying, didactic and interior tone. In brief, painting which was religious for the 16 th century. The monkish character of the Hieronymite of El Escorial —and of his wish to justify the orthodox tastes of the prudent king, which for certain mentalities of the time were heterodox— have led cri-

tics to doubt the «impartiality» of the comments in the «History of the Order of Saint Jerome». However, Sigüenza was no narrow-minded devout. It is true that he criticised religious paintings which did not move one to devotion or prayer (13), but his concept of art was not restricted to reducing its aims to the creation of pious images. His words in defence of the frescoes —with nudes— by Pelegrino Tibaldi in the El Escorial library are well-known and sprang from an open-minded sense of decorum and propriety. Sigüenza attempts to explain, of course, how Bosch's art is essentially religious and moral but, without a doubt, from a stance quite far removed from that which we might call traditional. Let us remember that the Hieronymite friar, a follower of the not so orthodox Bible scholar Benito Arias Montano and in the ultimate analysis an erasmist as was his master from Extremadura, was to suffer for his «advanced» ideas in an inquisitorial trial (1592), for he sustained doctrines and ideas far removed from those of the majority of his monastery companions. Perhaps a vague explanation of his enthusiasm for the work of Bosch is to be found in his attitude —still hypothetical, to a greater extent than in the case of Montano (14)— as a sympathiser with the ideas of the Flemish sect *Familia Chariatitis.* The family-based sect (15) was a late development of the celebrated Nordic spiritual movement which we know as the *devotio moderna* and, based on the idea of the insufficiency of human reason to understand the words of the Bible and of God, preached love, peace, humanity and charity in an obscure, symbolic style and considered itself to be above all existing churches and showed contempt for them. The internal religion of the familists was highly individualised, and it was established that each member of the sect sould keep in direct contact with God by hearing his inner voice. The affinities between these ideas and those of the friar from Sigüenza on the one hand, and those of Bosch and the *modern devout* of the end of the 15th century on the other, and even more as seen through the personal prism of the Hieronymite of El Escorial, may have justified the preference of this latter for the works of the former, which were at the same time both moralistic and critical of the traditional uses and abuses in religious and worldly matters, «written» in an obscure, allegorial language which would delight a euphuistic man such as Fray José de Sigüenza.

---

(13) Remember his comment on the *Martyrdom of St. Maurice* by El Greco (also in El Escorial), based on the «words» of the painter Juan Fernández Navarrete «the dumb». See Sigüenza. *op. cit.* II Part, III Book IV, discourse XVIII.

(14) Marcel Bataillon. *Erasmo y España.* Mexico, 1966, p. 743-8.

(15) Ben Reckers. *Arias Montano.* Madrid, 1973. p. 151 ff. On the *Familia Charitatis idem* p. 101 ff., and, above all, M. Rooses. *Christophe Plantin, imprimeur anversois.* Brussels, 1883.

During the following century —the 17th— Bosch's fame continued as did the interest in his work, Spain being one of the countries in which his painting met with greatest appreciation both in cultured and literary circles and in the popular strata. On the one hand, Bosch was popular among Spanish writers of the 17th century; on the other, his images linked up with the terrorific-burlesque tradition which the common people found so genial (16). Even the Aragonese painter Jusepe Martínez in his «Practicable Essays on the most Noble Art of Painting» (ca. 1675) (17), considered the painter of Hertogenbosch to be Toledan, although naturally trained in painting in Flanders. However, criticism of Bosch in the Iberian peninsula was to change with the turn of the century. Juan de Butrón, an outright defender of the art of painting as a liberal activity (18), appreciated his work, although he acknowledged that certain of his «caprices» might be taken for «lascivious». Francisco Pacheco, Velázquez's father-in-law and inquisitorial consultant on artistic matters, after a euphuistic discourse on painters of «crickets» and other «riparographers» and having judged Hieronymus Bosch's «caprices» as «ingenious» with «the variety of guises which be fashioned of the devils», passes sentence thus: (19)

«Father José de Sigüenza honours him too much, making those licentious fantasies mysterious, which we do not invite painters to do».

Sigüenza's critical approach was maintained (thus in Lope de Vega, who considerd Bosch to be a harbourer of philosophical moralities under the ridiculous and imperfect figures) (20), but the Fleming became increasingly viewed as a capricious painter, a paradigm of the licentious and fantastic. Bosch gradually became the prototype of the monstrous, the mysterious and horrifying, almost totally incomprehensible and meaningless but at the same time entirely orthodox from the Catholic religious point of view, despite his «licentious» licences. Even Francisco de Quevedo saw

(16) See Julio Caro Baroja. *Las formas complejas de la vida religiosa. Religión, sociedad y carácter en la España de los siglos XVI y XVII.* Madrid, 1978. p. 61 ff. On the Spanish tradition of the 15th century in horrific-burlesque works, see Isabel Mateo López. *Temas profanos en la escultura gótica española. Las sillerías de coro.* Madrid, 1979, with bibliography on this tradition abroad.

(17) Jusepe Martínez. *Discursos practicables del nobilísimo arte de la pintura.* ed. Julián Gallego, Barcelona, 1950.

(18) Juan de Butrón. *Discursos apologéticos en que se defiende la ingenuidad del arte de la pintura.* Madrid, 1626.

(19) Francisco Pacheco. *Arte de la pintura.* Seville, 1649. ed. F. J. Sánchez Cantón. Madrid, 1956.

(20) See, as for others of these quotations, Xavier de Salas. *El Bosco en la literatura española.* Barcelona, 1943. p. 30 ff.

him thus, who nicknamed the poet Góngora the «Bosch of poets» on account of his «monstrous style» and relegated the painter to Hell although he did not see him as an agnostic, unbeliever or heretic al all (21). Quevedo, who in turn was to call himself the «apprentice or second part of the atheist and painter Hieronymus Bosch» (22), was to put the following words into the mouth of a devil (23):

> «But leaving this to one side, I wish to tell you that we are very pained by the hashes you make of us, painting us with claws when we are not birds; with tails when there are tailed demons; with horns when we are not married, and scant-bearded, when there are devils amongst us who could be hermits and magistrates. You must remedy this, for only a short while ago Hieronymus Bosch went there and when he was asked why he had painted us in so many guises in his dreams, he replied that it was because he had never believed that there were any real demons.»

Like Giampaolo Lomazzo in the previous century, Quevedo once more looks for the root of his extravagant fantasies in dreams, comparing his caprices with the results of a suspension of the vision of the real world, of nature. This is doubtless a negative way of explaining it. In order to see Bosch with the same eyes with which we look at him now, it was necessary for the Renaissance and the Baroque to have occurred since his own time, and with the former Descartes and Calderón, and, with even greater reason, Romanticism, Comte, Freud and the surrealists. Thanks to all of them we have attained our present, and maybe on occasion erroneous, point of view of rather points of view.

In the specific field of the History of Art the change of orientation in the study of Bosch is due to Max Dvorák and the so-called Vienna School who saw in his spiritual content the chief centre of interest of these artistic manifestations rather than in the pure forms, the change of approach on the part of the spectator of his works is due to the psychoanalytical theory of Sigmund Freud and to the artistic phenomenon of contemporary surrealists who were greatly influenced by the Austrian

---

(21) See on this subject Helmut Heidenreich. «Hieronymus Bosch in some literary context». *Journal of the Warburg and Courtauld Institutes,* 1970. p.171-99. Heidenreich is against Salas's interpretation in *op. cit.* p. 31-4.

(22) Luis Pacheco de Narváez in *Tribunal de la Justa Venganza,* quoted in Francisco de Quevedo. *Obras completas,* ed. Luis Astrana Marin. Madrid, 1932. p. 1130 of the works in verse.

(23) Francisco de Quevedo in «El alguacil endemoniado». *Obras completas. ed. cit.* p. 144 of the prose works.

psychiatrist. Research and attempts to understand Bosch's work should be directed as has been done on different occasions along other paths: those of its thematic content and those of its intrinsic content, explained from the point of view of the assumptions in force among Bosch's contemporaries, and not from those of our own time. Research —and, if one gets there, understanding— should be directed through iconographic analyses of Bosch's artistic motifs which may be found in the literary sources of the time and the history of *types* (subjects or specific concepts expressed by objects or actions); through the study of the essential tendencies of the human mind conditioned by the artist's personal psychology and the *Weltanschauung* of his time; through the history of symbols in their precise sense of specific subjects and concepts which reflect the essential tendencies of the human mind (24); that is to say, through reality rather than through the fantastic imagination or, in other words, through the use of historical methods tempered, if possible, by common sense (25). However, this path has not always been followed and the researcher's steps have often faltered, the traveller often erring to heed tempting terrestrial sirens.

The divulgation of the naturalistic conception of human life on which Sigmund Freud's psychological theory is based, its formulation in terms of conscience/and unconsciousness/subconsciousness, his research into the meaning of dreams and oneiric symbology, on the one hand the dependence of man's behaviour on the human libido and on the other the use by the surrealists of the association of words and «daydreams» as feasible methods for artistic creation suggested by the therapeutic techniques of analysis, have led certain sectors of critics and some spectators of the Flemish painter's works to make use of this portion of their cultural baggage in the interpretation of Bosch's work.

Was the use of this type of methodology justifiable in an attempt to explain and decipher the work of the master of Hertogenbosch? The only qualities of his art which invite a psycho-analytical interpretation, perhaps, are their mysterious beauty and his «libidinous» symbolism; his strange and twisted towers might be taken as obvious phallic symbols, his ripe strawberries and pomegranates —full of seed— for natural acts

---

(24) Erwin Panofsky. *Estudios sobre iconología.* Madrid, 1972, Introduction.
(25) Erwin Panofsky. *Early Netherlandish Painting. Its Origins and Character.* New York, 1971. I, p. 142; in this case, on the existence or non-existence of «disguised» symbols of reality *(disguised symbolism)* or hidden ones.

THE GARDEN OF DELIGHTS *(frag.)*. Prado Museum, Madrid.

of procreation, the quiet ponds and pools which dot his landscapes could also suggest gestating fields. However, not all is sex by any means in Bosch. It could be that the application of the methods of Freudian psycho-analysis and Carl Jung's psychology are of great value in the interpretation of what Sigüenza calls the «macarronic» works of Bosch, or those which reveal to us the «inner man» —in another sense conscious and not unconscious— of the Spanish Hieronymite friar, but the attempts made so far have often been arbitrary and it is doubtful that the contenutistic and psychological secrets of Bosch's works might be revealed even by someone well-versed in both metholodogies, psychoanalytical and historico-artistic.

It is not of great interest to speculate on whether Jeroen van Aken, alias Bosch, suffered from neuroses, hallucinations or other mental disorders produced by one or another psychopathic state. Explanations of the ensemble of Bosch's work provided by psychologists are in principle further from the probable reality than those supplied by historians of art and late medieval culture. The decipherings of Bosch's symbols, whether isolated or interrelated, should be based above all on the study of the established representative traditions of his time, on specific litarary texts and living ideas —in a demonstrable way— of the historical period in question and those with which an artist would probably be familiar, on the existing possibilities that the interpretation fit in with the historical situation and personal tendencies of a master considered individually; that is, more on history than on the potential universality of a symbol.

As far as Bosch's surrealism is concerned (as likewise that of other artists considered to be surrealists *avant la lettre),* the very theorist of the movement, André Breton pointed out at one time that no continuity existed which could be organized as a surrealist tradition and argued that the vision of contemporary artists «could not in any way be set on the same level as those imaginary beings created by religious terror and escaped from the more or less perturbed reason of a Hieronymus Bosch. It is difficult, not to say impossible, to imagine Jeroen van Aken before a panel attempting to trace onto its pictorial surface images escaped from his dreams or extracted —consciously— from his own subconscious, putting into practice certain techniques of artistic creation which in many cases were considered scandalous and anti-aesthetic even in our own 20th century.

Despite any romantic concept which we might have on his «surrealism», Bosch should be studied and understood in the first place, as a Flemish artist who responds in an incredible way to the «psychosis» of his turbulent times, that Autumn of the Middle Ages which another Dutch painter, Johan Huizinga (26) portrayed so well. Bosch worked on totally different assumptions to those of the surrealist artists and with diametrically opposed aims and ends. If one was to talk of surrealism in Bosch, one would have to say that he forges it within the context of a well-defined religious iconography and that his images, both spontaneous and archetypal, must be viewed as part of the schemas of tradicional religious compositions. It is in the juxtaposition of traditional Christian iconography and his personal «oneiric» images, to call them by some metaphoric name, that we find those contradictions which make his work an enigma and a source of disconcertment. But are Bosch's images and symbols derived from a subconscious association? Are they the result of daydreaming? Many of Bosch's symbols and images have been explained in documented historical sources which come to certain precise conformations - precise in either idea or in form. However, others are still left unjustified and unxexplainable. Nevertheless, it is improbable that we could ever get to know the mental mechanisms set in action by Bosch to carry out his works, to construct his «crickets», his fantastic semi-human beings and semi-animal, semi-vegetable and semi-artificial ones. Bosch's mental structure will remain a hidden secret for ever although we may carry on deciphering some of his monsters or chimeras. But if the deciphered ones have been so done to on the basis of history and meticulous, erudite intellectual work supported by conscious elements and relationships, it is hard to think that they came out of their author's brain by subconscious means. In fact, as we have seen, when older criticism appealed to dreams, to the subconscious, it was an easy way out —by denial— of what could not be believed to be conscious for it appeared to be incomprehensible.

Explanations of Bosch's paintings have sprung from the most traditional moralistic and didactic interpretations, such as Sigüenza's, to go on to be enriched and even denied and finally, for critics, from time to time and after these «denials», to return to the original statements. Let us take, for example, perhaps the most representative of the critical itinerary of any of Bosch's works: the triptych of *The Garden of Deligths,* above

---

(26) Johan Huizinga. *El otoño de la Edad Media.* Madrid, 1965.

all its central panel. Even in our time, the moralizing interpretation of the Hieronymite from Sigüenza has been upheld with certain differences of meaning and, of course, with ever greater specifications as far as his partial meanings and details are concerned: on the outside, the world on the third day of Creation, Genesis still incomplete; on the inside, to the left, the creation of Eve, the origin of sin; on the central panel, the deadly sins; to the right, Hell as a punishment for sin. After the purely moralistic global explanation, partial codes have been used to interpret his symbolism, above all that of the enigmatic central panel of the triptych in Madrid. Combe (27) has turned to symbols used in contemporary alchemists' lore; Dirk Bax (28) has developed research of his «sexual» symbols based on folklore, sayings, linguistic wordplay and proverbs of the time; De Tolnay (29), whilst accepting the «moral» interpretation, has insisted upon a type of psycho-analytical explanation, the world as a representation of human dreams which tries to break the limits imposed on love by the morals and traditions in force at the time. For De Tolnay, Bosch would have used a symbology of an erotic type based on Macrobius's theory of dreams in his comment on the «Dream of Scipio the African» by Cicero and on the codification and repertoirs of oneiric symbols of the end of the 15th century, such as «Les songes de Daniel Prophète» (1482). According to this keen and intelligent art historian, Bosch would have tried to evoke in his works the result of the unconscious sleep of the human soul, tending to reconstruct the oneiric process perhaps in a conscious way just the opposite to the psychoanalyst who attempts to free the symbolic elements from dreams— as a vehicle of universal communication among all men and in a process which one might term psychosynthetic, as against the psychoanalytic one.

These interpretations are opposed by those which see in Jeroen van Aken a heretic or follower of esoteric sects. For Fraenger, the Adamite Jeroen van Aken painted in the central panel of the Prado triptych the sensual Paradise of his Adamite coreligionists, free of prejudice and frustrations and in intimate contact with the Godhead through spiritual and physical love; according to his theory, Hell would be converted into the Purgatory of the «heretics» who denied the sect of the «Brethren of

(27) J. Combe. *Jérôme Bosch*. Paris, 1946.
(28) Dirk Bax. «Beschrijving en poging tot verklaring van Het Tuin der Onkuisheid drieluik van Jeroen Bosch, gevold door kritiet op Fraenger». *Verhandelingen d. K. Nederlandse Academie van Wetenschappen,* 63, 2, 1956. p. 1-208.
(29) Charles De Tolnay. *Hieronymus Bosch,* Basle, 1937.

THE HAYCART *(frag.).* Prado Museum, Madrid.

the Free Spirit» (30). Wertheim-Aymés (31) made the right-hand panel into a Purgatory which leads on to the central panel, the nirvana of the joys of love. Such explanations are based on a minimum of true documentary data but their importance has become hypertrophied and, without bearing any true connection to Bosch at all, have been unfairly manipulated and even placed in close relationship to the painter to, according to them, «enable a clarification» of his works.

During the past years, after rejecting such interpretations meticulously and with good reasons, historians have returned to the older explanations armed with new historical arguments. Peter Glum (32) has pointed out the possibility of deciphering the central panel in Madrid as the world before the Last Judgement; Ernst H. Gombrich (33) has analyzed it as a moral allegory of the instability, transience and evanescence of the natural world, and, basing his argument on the title given to the picture in old inventories (34), as a representation of the antedeluvian world, a prefiguration of the blindness of the world in the face of the flood which the future universal Judgement consists of. For Gombrich, the outer grisaille —founded on Biblical texts and on Petrus Comestor (12th. cen.)'s «Historia Scholastica»— becomes an image of the «postdeluvian» world, flooded by the waters as a punishment for its sins but in which the rainbow of the Holy Alliance with God shines; the central panel represents the antedeluvian world, *situc erat in diebus Noe,* happy and carefree and totally alien to its fate in which men —*diluvium non timentes*— forget what might happen or what undoubtedly and ineluctably will happen next: the Flood; after this, the Last Judgement.

The history of culture in the Flanders of 1500, the history of criticism of the painter's work, the spiritual tendencies of his patrons (we shall discuss these later on) and of the original owners of his paintings (the church of St. John of Hertogenbosch, the parish church of Hocke near

---

(30) Wilhelm Fraenger. *Hieronymus Bosch: das Tausendjährige Reich.* Coburg, 1947; Eng. ed. London, 1952; French ed. Paris, 1966.
(31) C. A. Wertheim-Aymès. *Hieronymus Bosch, eine Einführung in seine geheime Symbolik* Amsterdan, 1957.
(32) Peter Glum. «Divine Judgement in Bosch's *Garden of Earthly Delights.*» The Art Bulletin, 1976, p. 45-54.
(33) Ernst H. Gombrich. *op. cit.*
(34) Ernst H. Gombrich. «Bosch *Garden of Earthly Delights:* A Progress Report.» *Journal of the Warburg and Courtauld Institutes,* 1969, p. 162-70. Thus is titled the copy or replica of the *Garden of Delights* which Archduke Albert possessed in Brussels in 1595.

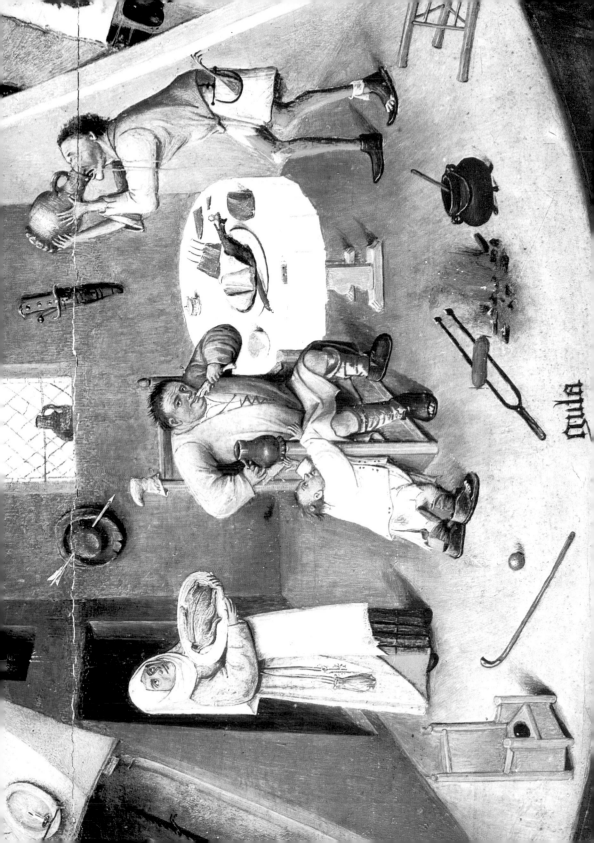

Bruges, the monastery of San Lorenzo el Real at El Escorial, Philip the Fair and his sisters, the ruler of the Low Countries Doña Margarita, Henry III of Nassau, Cardenal Grimani, the Bishop of Utrecht, the Portuguese painter Damiâo de Goes, Don Diego and Don Felipe de Guevara, Jean de Casembroot, the lord of Backerzeele, Philip II, the Spanish prior or the Order of St. John of Jerusalem, Don Fernando de Toledo, Archduke Albert, in the 16th century), should be the paths to follow, and so they have been on numerous occasions with the result that the work of the painter of Hertogenbosch has become well-known.

Yet, however, and as Erwin Panofsky (35), one of the greatest authorities on Flemish painting, has said, although many holes have been drilled in the door of a closed room, nobody has yet discovered to key to open it. Despite each and every one of the different holes made in the door, research on the scriptural exegesis, Flemish folklore, magic treatises, or those of alchemists, astrologists or on dreams, the masterkey is still to be found. The result is that many aspects of the figure and work of the painter still remain obscure, ambiguous and equivocal or inaccessible. Moreover, it is unfortunately probable that they will remain thus for a long time, perhaps for ever.

However, Bosch's genius towers unique above all the problems of interpreting his work, its details and biographical data still to be revealed, and has made him not only one of the greatest painters of European art but also one of the sources of western imagination. Before Bosch, there existed fantastic, symbolic or monstrous art, but it had never achieved a complexity, intensity, visual reality, numeric accumulation and originality comparable to those of our artist. The echo of his painting may be traced through literary sources from his own time —we have already discussed some of them— and naturally, this echo may be followed up in the works of his imitators, copiers and those masters influenced by his work and portentous imagination. Luke van Leyden, Quentin Massys, the Breughels, Jan de Cock, Jan Mandyn, Peter Huys, Brouwer, Teniers, Jacques Callot, Luke Cranach, to quote just a few of the most important painters, bear good witness to this.

Even for us today, on many occasions the fantastic is often connected with his name and we see and re-imagine the fantastic, the monstrous, the outlandish, the horrifying, the supernatural, the malign and the

(35) E. Panofsky. *Early* ...... I, p. 357.

demoniac through images taken from the repertoir offered by his paintings. Thus, from the comments of Philip II on the demons in a procession in Lisbon 1582, which he addressed to his sons by letter: «... there were some demons which looked like the paintings of Hieronymus Box whom I think he was frightened of (Prince Philip) ... they were a sight and could be seen from afar and looked more like things of Hieronymus Boces than devils. And it is true that they were well-made, for they were not real ones» (36), to the strange, amusing beings, which, as though they had been taken from the palette of an optimistic and jovial Bosch, rampaged across the cinema screen only a few years ago in the showing of *The Yellow Submarine* (37).

This inventive capacity, this prodigious imagination —and not only in the fantastic but also in the representation of the everyday— is what above all attracts us, even more than whatever his fantastic forms might mean; the appeal, slightly primitive and archaic, of the unintelligible, but at the same time and maybe more markedly so on account of this, the tangible, the close, the almost real on account of its naturalistic configuration almost with the qualities of really perceived images. Bosch, like very few artists, was able to fulfill the two requisites, apparently contradictory, which turn the vision into a work of art. On the one hand, he is a past-master of «naturalism» for only when one contemplates a world controlled by the laws of Nature can one have any awareness of the suspensión of those laws, of their suppression, which is the essence of the «miracle». On the other hand, Bosch is able to transfer the miraculous event from the level of factuality to that of an imaginative experience (38). Thus his fantastic visions not only his detailed symbolic forms— take on a value as realities despite the «errors» of naturalistic representation and the poetic licence which one may observe in his works. These latter in their ensemble stand before us not only as imaginative repertoirs of mysterious and esoteric symbolisms, but as true works of art. Thus his landscapes, desolate and swept by the winds of destruction, fragile and brittle as transparent egg-shells, hard as rocks of unknown minerals or fertile fields filled with sheaves, streams, woods and trees and fantastic or real cities, also become examples of the greatest formal beauty ever attained in this difficult pictorial genre. Thus, too, his scenes

---

(36) X. de Salas. op. cit. p. 11-2.
(37) Cartoon film directed by George Dunning, with music by «The Beatles».
(38) Erwin Panofsky. *The Life and Art of Albrecht Dürer*. Princeton, 1971. p. 55-6.

from everyday life, full of the charm of what he lived and experienced personally, although they be portrayals of vice and sins, move us rapidly by their direct nature. For eventually, and despite everything, although we understand little or nothing of what is shown before our eyes, we shall always be faced with the works of an undecipherable and incomprehensible artist although one who is oustandingly and brilliantly great, a totally exceptional artist. Form prevails over the information which any painting might offer us and this is what makes a painting, as likewise any other «aesthetic» manifestation, a work of art.

II
JEROEN VAN AKEN

We know precious little that is certain about the figure of Jeroen van Aken, the man who was to sign his paintings as Hieronymus Bosch. Despite the tremendous search carried out in the archives of his home town for biographical details of his person (and which have suppied *news* at least up to 1967 (1), the limited number of documentary data which we possess about his life removes the real man far from the complex, mysterious, tortured and tortuous image which could be the reflection of his personality in the mirror of his artistic output. For those who expect a biography of the painter in accordance with what he offers us at first sight in his paintings, the reality must of necessity be a disappointment for in his personal and private life the only mysterious element springs from our own lack of knowledge.

Jeroen van Aken was born in Hertogenbosch (Bois-le-Duc) on the 2nd of October, 1453, if we follow the suggestion resulting from Mosmans research (2). The limits for the dates of his birth had traditionally been accepted as between the years 1450 and 1455, and even as late as 1460. Although Mosmans has not offered any concrete evidence to confirm his suggested chronology, no documentary evidence has as yet been published which would contradict or refute his dates. It is quite possible that, should his surname have had a topographical origin or should it have been a toponym, then his family came from Aix-la-Chapelle but, if this is true, when Jeroen was born in the Brabantine town this latter would already have become emancipated from the old Carlovingian capital, for the Aken's move to Hertogenbosch would then date

---

(1) P. Gerlach. «Jeronimus van Aken alias Bosch en de Onze Lieve Vrouwe-Broederschap». *Bijdragen bij gelegenheid van de herdenkingstentoonstelling te's-Hertogenbosch,*1967. p. 48-60. «Studies over Jeronimus van Aken (alias Bosch)». *Spiegel der Historie,* 1967. p. 587-98 and p. 623-70.
(2) J. Mosmans. *Jheronimus Anthoniszoon van Aken alias Hieronymus Bosch,* Hertogenbosch, 1947.

from several generations back. His paternal grandfather, Jan van Aken, carried on a renowned artistic activity in this city. There also, his maternal grandfather's quiet tailor's life was spent.

His grandfather Jan's artistic profession, although bordering the sphere of craftsmanship, must to a great extent have marked the life of his descendents. Jeroen's father, Anthonis van Aken and two of his uncles Gossen and Thomas must also have been artists. Jeroen had five brothers and sisters: Anthonis, Jan, Katherine, Heberta and Gossen. This latter was to inherit his father's workshop and therefore should be considered as the eldest or at least as older than Jeroen and possibly also occupied in some artistic activity.

As regards Bosch's childhood and adolescence, we have no news whatsoever. Unfortunately, neither do we possess any about his artistic apprenticeship. With no knowledge at all of any master in whose workshop he may have learnt the trade of painter nor any proof whatsoever on his hypothetical absence from his home town as a result of training away from Hertogenbosch, we have no other alternative but to conjecture —on the other hand, quite logically— a probable training in his father's workshop or in that of one of his uncles for his grandfather Jan had died in the year of our painter's birth. Thus, as we shall later see again, the artist's training must have been carried out far from the Flemish artistic centres of the time, in a provincial environment which kept on the margin of the innovating developments of other centres such as Brussels, Bruges or Haarlem. Round about 1480 or 1481, Bosch must have been awarded the grade of master within the hierarchic organization of his guild. In fact on the 3rd. January 1481 a certain *Jeronimus pictor* appears signing a public document thus in which he gives over part of a house in Hertogenbosch to his brother Gossen, a house situated precisely in the *Grande Place,* the main square or market of the city of Brabant. However, some historians, lacking data on a painters'guild in his home town and as there was no record of Bosch as a «master», have doubted that Jeroen ever attained this «academic» grade and that his artistic activity was bound within the type of hierarchic organization of a markedly institutional and economic nature such as that of the guilds.

The first three documents in which Jeroen appears all belong to the eighth decade of the century and are therefore prior to that of 1481 mentioned above, being of a similar type. The third, however, displays a slight-

ly different tone. The first dated 5th April 1474, shows us Katherine, her brothers (among whom is Jeroen) and her father taking part in a financial transaction regarding the lease of a small plot of land. In the second of July 26th 1474, Anthonis and his son sign a debit-note to a certain Jan Goyart Noyen. In the third, of an uncertain date between 1475 and 1476, Anthonis and his sons are present at the adjudication of an altarpanel for the Brotherhood of Our Lady of Hertogenbosch to the sculptor Adrian van Wesel. This is, then, the first document in which Bosch is seen as vinculated to the artistic life of his town, the witness of a sculpture contract subscribed by another artist. In 1481, or maybe 1480, Bosch *(Jeroen de maelre,* Hieronymus the painter) signed a new document, regarding his artistic activity: Bosch acquired two compartments of the old altar-piece of the Brotherhood of Our Lady which his father had left without painting.

About the same time Bosch appears for the first time as married to Aleyt, the daughter of Goyart van de Mervenne, to whom he may have been married around 1478. Aleyt was born in 1453 and was the daughter of Goyart, called Brandt, and Postellina, daughter in turn of a chemist and who had died in 1472. Jeroen's father-in-law was a man of good social and economic status and Aleyt brought to the marriage a dowry of land in Oirschot. We know that Jeroen had to see to these small estate properties as he intervened several times on different occasions in financial transactions regarding them, or for other economic causes regarding his wife's property. Thus we see him in 1482 (llth April), 1483 (3rd January and 21st March), in 1487 (29th December), 1488 (lst October), 1492 (7th February), 1494 (6th March) and 1498 (17th May and 30th July). These petty affairs —maybe important for the couple— were to be the cause of certain family disputes between the couple and Goyart van de Mervenne. His real estate, on the other hand, was increased in 1484 thanks to an inheritance from his brother-in-law Goerdt, a small plot of land known as *ten Roedenken,* also in Oirschot. Bosch and his wife also possessed urban property for in 1488 (23rf and 26th February) they sold a small house belonging to them in the *Scilderstraetke* (painter's lane) and in 1507/8 they had to pay rates as the owners, or maybe only as the tenants, of a house in the *Grande Place* of Hertogenbosch, a tax levied on account of the war against the Duchy of Guelders.

Judging from the taxes which he paid during the course of his life and which would mean that he kept two servants in his house (according to a document of 1510), Jeroen van Aken's economic situation must have been comfortable and Bosch was to work until his death —and above all, as from his marriage— free from the type of economic problems which so often plague artists and not only those of his own time. This comfortable economic situation and his high social status through his marriage perhaps allowed him to carry out a freer and more independent activity than average and gave him the opportunity to express his ideas regarding the Church and other sectors of contemporary society, ideas which were not always orthodox and most often critical, in a way which would have been vetoed or limited had Bosch not been in these precise personal circumstances.

If his family of artists and marriage to Aleyt are two important factors in Bosch's vital development, so also is his relationship with a religious institution of Hertogenbosch, to which we have already seen the painter vinculated from 1475/6. We refer to the Brotherhood of Our Lady *(Lieve Vrouwe Broederschap)* in the now cathedral of Saint John which then had no more than collegiate status and which was a pious institution and formed the core of our artist's biography. Jeroen van Aken entered the Brotherhood of Our Lady in 1486 or 1487 and was to be a member of it until his death. Bosch took an active part in the life of this brotherhood and appears on several occasions quoted in the documents preserved in its old archives (for example, he appears registered as a member in the years 1488, 1489, 1493, 1498, 1503, 1508 and 1512). We also know that in 1487 or 1488 he donated a sum of money to the brotherhood and that during this latter year he presided the «swan banquet» which the brethren held regularly, a banquet which was to be repeated in 1498 or 1510 (on the 10th March to be precise) Jeroen invited the members of the brotherhood to his house for a meal upon the occasion of the funeral of the knight and member Jan Backx. Bosch also worked on several occasions on the decoration of the chapel which the brotherhood possessed in the collegiate church and even painted certain minor works commissioned by certain of its members.

The Brotherhood of Our Lady, founded in 1318, seems to have been one more of the countless brotherhoods and confraternities of the religious type that existed in the Medieval world and still do in the modern one. Some of these were of guild origin, some grew out of a special devotion and devoted their efforts to promoting the religious life of their members and to directing and encouraging pious and charitable behaviour in their members. Thus, the Brotherhood of Our Lady centred its activities during the 15th century on works of charity after almost a century of existence in which the chief mission of the brotherhood had been tasks connected with the cult, particularly with the Marian cult under whose invocation and protection it had been created. This change of direction or, at least, the intensification of this type of activities must have been the result of the influence of the Bretheren of the Common Life, a congregation which has often been quoted as a hypothetical source of inspiration for Jeroen's religious feelings either through the brotherhood itself and personal contact with the bretheren, or more directly thorough the literary works of contemporary Flemish mysticism to which they subscribed and had in fact imbued with their spirit in the particular type of religiousness of the so-called «Hieronymites».

This Common Life congregation had been founded in 1381 by Geert Groote (1340-1384), a disciple of the hermit and mystic Jan van Ruysbroeck (1293-1381) and one of the initiators of the new Christian spiritualist current which was termed *devotio moderna.* Towards 1500, some one hundred and fifteen «hieronymite» communities existed in the Low Countries: two of them had settled in Hertogenbosch during the century (in 1424 and 1480), in one of which the later universally renowned humanist Erasmus of Rotterdam was to reside for three years, the Dutchman who was to play such an important part in the religious life of Europe of the beginning of the 16th century. The Brethren of the Common Life spread a new spirit of religious life which on the one hand was implied in the struggle against heretical sects flourishing in Flanders at the time and, on the other, in the battle against the internal corruption of the clergy, both regular and secular. For them, a world converted into a theatre of sin and heresy was in need of a purer and more intimate union with God, one more personal and interiorized. Although this meant placing oneself without the pale of the offical church or of the traditional religious orders. Their attitude was of a clearly reformist nature; after the Lutheran reform, they came to be considered as «pre-reformists», «pre-Lutherans» and their followers were often mixed up —as is the case of many of the Spanish Erasmists— with true Protestants.

However, there is no doubt of the contrast, almost opposition, which exists between the fantastical, complex and tortuous work of Bosch and the serene, simple and intimist piety upheld and preached by the followers of the *devotio moderna,* who preached and practised a pure and simple love of God, and contrition rather than the attrition to which

THE CROWNING OF THORNS. *(frag.)*. National Gallery, London.

Bosch's paintings invite us. If the work of an artist should reflect the man behind them, it does not seem possible that we may identify the author of so many infernal visions with a «modern devout» who kept as bedside reading the most representative text of this current of thought, the «Imitatio Christi» by Thomas de Kempis (ca. 1379-1471).

But if one sector of Bosch's critics have seen in Jeroen's participating in the life of the Brethren of Our Lady —influenced by the brethren of the Common Life— a pre-Lutheran Bosch concerned with bringing about a new form of Christian existence in the world and with fighting the clergy and laymen of his time, other sectors have even offered and antipodal image of him or, as we shall see, several images totally opposed to the first.

These new images coincide with each other in showing us a heterodox Bosch from both a religious and aesthetic point of view, even a heretical one: a neo-Platonic Bosch, a Jeroen as a member of the Rosicrucian sect, or followers of the doctrine of Christian Rosencreuz (dead in 1484 but whose ideological wake was not to be overcome until the 17th century (3), an «Adamite» painter or, at least, in the service of the Adamite sect. Of all these, it is this latter theory which has caused greatest impact on the history of Bosch studies, although today most critics have basically rejected it even though they have not discarded elements contributed by the defenders of a detailed analysis of Bosch's symbolism.

Wilhelm Fraenger (4), the best-known and most illustrious of the sympathizers of the «Adamite» Bosch theory, based his interpretation of the Brabantine painter's work on the hypothesis of a close relationship between this latter and the *Homines Intelligentiae* sect, a satellite organization of the clandestine heresy of the Brothers and Sisters of the Free Spirit, also known under the name of Adamites. This heresy, condemned by Ruysbroeck himself around 1330, had appeared in the 13th century and spread widely during the 15th through Germany and the Netherlands in particular. However, towards the end of this century, its field of action seems to have become considerably restricted and there is no news of its existence in the region of Brabant during the life of Jeroen van Aken.

---

(3) C. A. Wertheim Aymès, *op. cit.*
(4) W. Fraenger. *op. cit.* W. Hollmann. *«Eine Deutung des Bildes» das Steinschneiden. Psyche, eine Zeitschrift für Tiefenpsychologie und Menschenkunde*, 5, 1951, p. 385 ff.

ECCE-HOMO. Stadelsches Museum, Frankfurt.

The Brethren of the Free Spirit based their doctrine on the aprioristic belief that both good and evil depend exclusively on Divine Will (an absolute denial of Free Will as maintained by Chistian orthodoxy, philosophic scholasticism and later Trentine Catholicism) and that therefore, man cannot deserve eternal life through his own merits. Humanity, in consequence, was destined to eternal salvation and thè existence of Hell was a fable rather than a pure entelechy. For the Adamites, the repression of sin (predestined to occur) was worse than the sin itself; the resurrection of the body did not exist; preaching, priests and sacramental penitence were a mere waste of time if they were not impositions in the interests of the clergy. The sexual act, among other things, was, according to their ideas, a Paradisiac pleasure and a deflowered woman had nothing to envy a virgin, nor should she feel beneath her in merits or esteem. The union of pleasure and love, both sensual and spiritual, was the best means of re-establishing the innocence lost in Eden, the original hermaphrodite identity of Adam who contained Eve within himself and with her the female beginning. This was the identity of the Adam who had not yet lost his rib at divine hands. From this desire for primal innocence, even prior to the apparition of Eve in Paradise and the Fall and Expulsion from Paradise, the cult to Adam was to be derived, and hence its name of «Adamite». From this innocence, from the ultimate bisexual identity of Adam was to flow the redemption of the human race and the new Paradise.

These ideas have come down to us through the acts of a trial which took place in 1411 before the court of the Bishopry of Cambrai and in which a certain Aegidius Cantor gave evidence, a layman and illiterate person. There is no doubt about the existence of such a heretical sect in the Lower German-Flemish Middle Ages but there are doubts about the organization of a sect in the strict sense of the word, that is, of an organized congregation of believers. There are no witnesses of the existence of degrees-novices, initiates, masters among its followers neither are there to the effect that these latter used a language and liturgical practices of an esoteric type. Neither have we any information as to the location of the Adamites in the region of Hertogenbosch during Bosch's lifetime.

As we lack any documentation to support such a thesis, it is difficult to accept it (5). It does not allow us to justify the differences —quite ob-

---

(5) D. Bax. *Ontcijfering van Jeroen Bosch.* The Hague, 1948 and «Beschrijving en poging tot verklaring van Het Tuin der Onkuisheid-drieluik van Jeroen Bosch, gevolgd door kritiek op Fraenger».

vious ones on the other hand— which exist between Bosch's works on religious themes and his large triptyches. We can only assume them to be different types of commissions. On the one hand, the former must have been painted by our artist for an ecclesiastic clientèle (6); on the other, the latter must have been done for the sect of the Free Spirit. In these latter, the heretical element would have been camouflaged into a forest of fantastic extravagances which would confound the non-initiated spectator or, on account of their significant ambiguity, might be interpreted by the profane as orthodox works.

However, as we have no documented knowledge (we shall speak later of this) of the painter's clients, Fraenger originally identified the hypothetical Grand Master of the Adamites, Bosch's spiritual patron and mentor, as a hypothetical Italian who was skilled in all arts derived from Florentine Neoplatonism. Later (7) he connected him with a tangible historical personage with whom Jeroen van Aken was probably in direct contact. The new Grand Master would have then been the Jew Jacob de Almaengien. This latter had been baptised in Hertogenbosch in 1494 (in the presence of the Duke of Burgundy Philip the Fair, the future Philip I King of Spain upon marriage to Princess Juana the Mad) and, after this date under his new name of Philippe van Sit Jans, also became a member of the Brotherhood of Our Lady, only to end up by returning to the Jewish faith ten years later. Despite the encarnation of the Adamite Master in a historical personage of flesh and blood, there are no proofs which connect him with the heretical sect nor which show him to be the owner of the series of esoteric knowledge which he transmitted to the painter.

In any case, the surest thing is that Bosch and Philippe van Sit Jans knew each other and met each other with a certain assiduity. We can indeed see in the double renegade a source of knowledge for our painter, yet however this is a knowledge which is far less esoteric and fantastic than has been supposed. Jacob de Almaengien may have been a source, or even partially responsible, for the undeniable familiarity with which

<hr>

Verhandelingen d.K. Nederlandse Academie van Wetenschappen, 63, 2, 1956. p. 1-208. J. Mosmans. *Jheronimus Bosch: Maria en Sint Jan, unbekend en laat schilderwerk bewaard in zijne vaderstad.* Hertogenbosch, 1950.
(6) Or deprived of orthodox religious nature.
(7) W. Fraenger. *op. cit.* and «Hieronymus Bosch: *Der verlorene Sohn*». *Castrum Peregrini,* 1 Amsterdam, 1951. p. 27-39.

Bosch dealt with and handled material from Jewish legends and customs (8).

Another member of the Brotherhood of Our Lady with whom Bosch must have been on friendly terms and who could have influenced him is the sculptor and architect Allaert de Hameel, This artist, who was to engrave some of the painter's works such as the *Last Judgement* and an *Elephant in Battle,* was a member of the Brotherhood during his stay in Hertogenbosch, which occurred between 1478 and 1494. During this period of time Allaert directed the works of the south wing of the transept of the collegiate church of St. John and began those of the central nave. The grotesque, demoniac figures on the rampant arches above the choir of the building and on its flying buttresses, which on the other hand are quite normal in medieval ecclesiastic decoration as from pre-Romanesque times, have on several occasions been judged as one of the possible sources of inspiration for our painter.

Another aspect of Bosch's life on which contemporary documents supply us with valuable information, although unfortunately less than necessary, is that of his work. Thus his first documented works (today missing although known through copies) were to be the outsides of the side panels of the triptych in the chapel of the Brotherhood of Our Lady, decorated with the Biblical episode of *Abigail and David.* We know that the sculptor Adriaen van Wessel of Utrecht had worked on the central panel between 1475/6 and 1477 and that in 1480/1 Bosch himself acquired two panels of the old altarpiece of the Brotherhood, panels which his father had left without painting. Between 1488 and 1492, Jeroen van Aken occupied himself with the painting of the outer wings, which were to be added in 1488/9 by Goyart Cuper. The inner sides, with *Solomon and Bathsheba* as iconographic subject, were recorded between 1521 and 1523 by the artist Gielis van Hedel of Brussels, called van de Bosch and who, it is thought, was a relation or follower of Bosch (9). Nevertheless, there has also been speculation and quite rightly (10) that the inner sides were also the work of the painter of Hertogenbosch and that van Hedel merely restored and repainted the panels. However this may be, the four original scenes were lost.

---

(8) See some of the types of this knowledge in Lotte Brand Philip. «The Prado *Epiphany* by Jerome Bosch». *The Art Bulletin,* xxxv, 4, 1953.

(9) M. J. M. Ebeling. «Jheronimus van Aken» *Miscellanea Gessleriana.* Antwerp, 1948. p. 444-57.

(10) Charles De Tolnay. *Hieronymus Bosch.* Baden-Baden, 1965. (on his work in Basle, 1937).

The next of his works to be documented dates from 1493/4. On the 7th February of one of these two years, Jeroen agreed to carry out a drawing on canvas as a model for the stained-glass window of the chapel of his Brotherhood, which was to be traced onto glass by the glass-maker Henricken Bueken around the same time. Ten years later, around 1503/4, there is a payment to Bosch by the Brotherhood so that this latter should paint or reproduce three scenes commissioned by the knights Jan Backx, Heinrich Massereels and Luke van Erpe.

The following commission documented in 1504 is of much greater importance. According to a document of the archives of Lille (France), Bosch received around that time the sum of thirty-six pounds in payment for a painting (9 x 11 feet in dimesion) of the *Last Judgement,* with Paradise and Hell, a painting commissioned by Philip the Fair *«pour son très-noble plaisir».* The destination of the triptych paid for in September 1504 is unknown although it has been supposed that this was the *Last Judgement* in the Vienna Akademie or, on a firmer basis, that part of it are the fragments of the *Judgement* in the Alte Pinakothek in Munich (11).

Another intervention of Bosch's occurred in 1508/9. The priors of the Brotherhood of Our Lady once more asked our artist for advice together with the architect of their chapel, Jan Heynste (or Heyns) as to the way in which to gild and polychrome the altarpiece, inviting both to give information of the final results of the work once it was finished by artists whose names we do not know. In 1511/2, Jeroen designed a cross and crucifix as a model for an image in terracotta, also commissioned by the Brotherhood. Lastly, in 1512/3, Bosch made a new model with same consignee, this time for a candlestick to be cast.

Another work for which Jeroen van Aken had to carry out at least the design and which was probably a commission from the collegiate church of Hertogenbosch, is that composed of two canvases with the *Virgin and Child* and *St. John the Evangelist,* which are currently preserved in the cathedral of this city. They were stuck onto the backs of the doors of a

---

(11) De Tolnay supposes that the Vienna triptych was a model or old copy of the altarpiece commissioned by Philip the Fair, basing his argument among other data, on the apparition of St. James of Compostelle (with St. Bavon) on one of the outer grisailles. Philip King of Castille at the death of Isabella the Catholic, may have chosen this iconography of the Spanish patron saint in homage to his wife, Queen Juana the Mad, and to the country in which he was to reign and quite soon to die.

large clock dated in 1513 and carried the inscription, perhaps apocry-phal ones: «*ISB*» and «*Bosch delineavit et p(in)xit*». Despite this caption and its bad state of preservation, it has been thought that these are work-shop works, carried out on a model supplied by the master.

Although some of these commissions may seem strange on account of their minor nature (a clock, a candle-stick, an image, etc.) and the im-portance which the painter has for us, this was common practice at the time. Anyone who is superficially familiar with the activities of medieval and modern painters as a whole, not only in their large works preserved in museums, will know of countless cases of distinguished artists taking on works of a minimun category and artistic importance.

On the other hand, we are also told of commissions (although not do-cumented or with their contacts and payments recorded) carried out by Bosch by the apparition of donors portrayed in his paintings, or in certain cases, of heraldic shields which tell us of the noble family that acted as client to the painter. Thus we find works commissioned by a laic clientèle of a private nature although the paintings have religious themes. Al-though not many of these works are preserved, those which have come down to us give us a good idea of the quite normal contractual environ-ment in which Bosch moved and also of the fact that these commissions cover, from the chronological point of view, practically the whole of the artist's active life. Early works such as *The Marriage in Canaan* in Rotter-dam (1475/80), the *Ecce Homo* in Frankfurt (1480/5, with the figures rubbed out but which are given by some of the captions on the panel) or the *Crucifixion* in Brussels (1480/5), have or had patrons. Other works are of a later date such as the Venetian altarpiece of *Saint Julia* (1500/4, with the figures rubbed out and repainted but still visible with the aid of X-rays), the *Last Judgement* in Vienna (after 1504 (?), with white shields on the outer grisailles) or the triptych of the *Epiphany* in Madrid (ca. 1510). The donors portrayed in the wings of this altarpiece have been identified as Pieter Bronckhorst and Agnes Bosshuyse (the ones who appear on the outer grisaille must be relations of theirs). The praying fi-gures in the Boston *Ecce Homo* have also been identified as members of the van Oss family of Hertogenbosch. In this polemical work (its date is problematic and there are critics who believe it to be a workshop pain-ting) the emblem of the «lily among thorns» curiously appears, which is characteristic of the Brotherhood of Our Lady. As we have already seen, not only the brotherhood of the Church of St. John acted as an institution

as the painter's client but also some of its members privately. We have also already spoken of the old owners of some of Bosch's paintings, who may also have been his clients more or less directly.

After having gone over the thread of Jeroen van Aken's biography as it is based on the data supplied by documents, we are faced with the existence of a blank period. Between 1499 an 1503/4 a documentary void occurs which is no less odd on account of the scant number of documents we know of on Bosch. Of course, this is not the only gap in his biography; others are those of 1477/80; 1484/6, 1489/91, 1505/6 and 1514/5. However, that of 1500-1503/4 most pressingly draws our attention. This period finishes in a blank with the most important known contract in the whole of the artist's life, the altarpiece for Duke Philip the Fair on the one hand; on the other, it marks the beginning of what was to be considered Italian influences on Bosch's work and Boschian influences on Italian art. In the third place, as from 1504, Flemish documents begin to add the alias of Bosch to his name Jeroen van Aken, Hieronymus Bosch a toponymic form abbreviated which he had already used as a signature on some of his works. This use of a toponym has been interpreted as the result of a trip abroad, to be precise to Italy (12) and, especially, to Venice. At a very early date works of the painter of Hertogenbosch appear there and the Italian influences on his work seem to come from Venetian art as we shall see below, or from northern Italian artists whose presence in the city of canals is recorded around the beginnings of the century. The most important case is that of Leonardo da Vinci, in whose drawings there appears a world of caricatures, of physiognomical studies and even of small pseudo-anthropormorphous monsters which may be the result of influence from the Flemish painter's art or, on the contrary, a source for our artist. Another element adduced in favour of the transalpine journey is the triptych of *Saint Julia* in Venice (13), a work datable between 1500 and 1504.

The altarpiece of the Palazzo Ducale in Venice, which has been in Italy for at least a couple of centuries, should its subject be confirmed, takes up the scene of the Crucifixion of a saint, Julia, in its central panel. The devotion to this saint was very rare but was located in two zones of

---

(12) Leonard J. Slatkes. «Hieronymus Bosch and Italy». *The Art Bulletin,* 1975. p. 335-45.

(13) For other historians and scholars of Bosch's work, this would not be the martyrdom of this Portuguese saint but of St. Liberata, *Virgo Fortis,* Ontcommer or Oncomer. If this iconography is confirmed, the hypothesis of the trip to Italy would lose one of its strongest points of support.

the Italian peninsula and its islands: Corsica and Brescia, above all in this latter city of the Po Valley. The recent discovery of two donors, afterwards repainted and substituted by two figures, in the side panels, dressed in the Italian fashion together with certain stylistic details, have led critics to think that this triptych was not only carried out by Bosch for certain Italian clients and for their home town, but also that it was even painted in Italy. Although so far the transalpine journey by Bosch —as any other trip within the Netherlands— is no more than mere hypothesis, this journey nevertheless which has no precendents among Flemish artists of the 15th century (14), would allow us to explain a series of iconographic and formal characteristics of the painter's art which so far have been only partly justifiable.

Few data can be added to complete Jeroen van Aken's recorded biography (15), if we make exception of his death. Bosch must have died a few days before the 9th August 1516, for on this day solemn funeral rites were held in the chapel of the collegiate church of Hertogenbosch for the «defunct brother Hieronymus of Aix-la-Chapelle, alias Bosch the renowned painter». This note on the archives speaks of the high esteem which Jeroen had enjoyed among his companions of the Brotherhood of Our Lady and, we suppose, among his fellow citizens.

With the death of Bosch reality ends and the legend surrounding his personality begins, a legendary character already noted in the texts of his first biographers, Felipe de Guevara (ca. 1560/2), D. Lampsonius (1572) or Karel van Mander (1604) (16) and one which was to be kept alive practically until the end of last century and still prevails even today. Let us return, however, to the data supplied by the archives, the only certain information at our disposal at present.

Jeroen van Aken appears to us a man whose life passes in a totally normal manner, restful, quiet, perhaps even monotonous in a home without children, without money problems, at his wife's side, between work in his workshop and the pious meetings of his devout and prestigious Brotherhood of Our Lady. Perhaps far from the hassle of more or less

---

(14) Other Flemish artists who travelled to Italy were Roger van der Weyden, Just de Gante, and probably, Hugo van der Goes.

(15) We also know that Jan van Aken, Jeroen's brother, died in 1498/9.

(16) D. Lampsonius. *Pictorum aliquot celebrium Germaniae effigies.* Antwerp, 1572. Carel van Mander. *Het Schilder-Boeck.* Haarlem, 1604.

THE TEMPTATIONS OF ST. ANTHONY. *(frag.).* Prado Museum, Madrid.

prolonged journeys, leading a routine life, seeing to his work and to his small family affairs in a small provincial town like Hertogenbosch. Only the most daring hypotheses have drawn a veil of mystery around his person as a reflection of the panels on their author, which puts in doubt the little we know about the artist. No conclusive evidence exists as to his familiarity with gnostic, orphic neoplatonic mysteries. In view of what we know for certain about him, it is difficult to think of Bosch, a respected citizen of a small provincial town and for thirty years an irreproachable member of a tremendously respecteble religious brotherhood, as a person who could have belonged —and worked for— an esoteric *club* of heretics who believed in a mixture of sex, mystic illumination and nudism. As Edwin Panofsky has pointed out (17), Bosch seems to us, more than a heretic, to be one of those extreme moralists who, obsessed by what they are fighting against, are fascinated, not without a certain pleasure, by visions of unheard of obscenities, perversions and tortures. The favourite painter of Philip II —together with Titian— perhaps might have experienced greater satisfaction watching an attractive heretic being burned at the stake than in joining her in her ascent into paradisiac joy. Perhaps, «like Philip II himself, Bosch could have been a case for psychoanalysis, but not one for the Inquisition». However this may be, even this image, which is probably nearer to his own real one, is far removed from convincing us altogether. There are elements in his work, and what may be deduced from his portrait in the codex of the Bibliothèque de la Ville d'Arras («Recueil d'Arras»), which could refute the idea of a Bosch full of obsessions, bent on preoccupations of a purely moral order and on denouncing spiritual corruption among his contemporaries. His mocking vision of life, his humour, his «being above it all», in sum, his scepticism, contradict the image of an implacable rigourist. Maybe we should discover when we weigh these suspicions a man who was «blasé» in the attitudes of certain disillusioned intellectuals, sceptics who are pessimists by intellection and optimists by vocation.

But to consider Bosch as an intellectual shut away in Hertogenbosch is another problem. If we accepted all the knowledge given as «literary sources» or as experiential ones for his work as though the painter himself had possessed them, there would be no other outlet but to come to the conclusion that he was an encyclopaedia of his time. His familiarity with orthodox Christian theology and ancient and medieval religious lite-

---

(17) E. Panofsky, *Early...*, p. 357.

rature (from the Bible to the «Ars Moriendi» through the apocryphal evangelists and the «Golden Legend» by Jacques de Voragine), whether this latter be «historical», hagiographic, edifying or fantastically terrifying (as the «Visio Tundali», among other texts), his knowledge of the popular and occult sciences (astrology, alchemy, demonology and witchcraft), of mosaic legends, native folklore, proverbial and popular wisdom, etc., all these would show him to be an encyclopaedic and omniscient painter, the possessor of a vast culture. Was this possible? While we can only speculate on Jeroen van Aken's reading (18) and some historians attempt to restrict his literary sources enormously to the Bible (19), we have no reply to our question. We may speculate, and men will continue to speculate, upon his knowledge but so far, as we have pointed out, nobody has found the key —or keys— which would completely decipher Bosch's work satisfactorily and it is unlikely that this key will be found.

If Jeroen van Aken's biography, or his external life as reflected in the public documents of the archives, may have been left clear of clouds of unknowing, Bosch's intellectual life, his inner life as reflected in his work, will remain veiled. And the greatest problem is not merely that of the «Open Sesame» key which would allow us to decipher his work, if it should at any time be found, but how to explain the mental mechanisms which, consciously or unconsciously, transformed certain given literary sources in a spectacular display of imagination in Bosch's pictorial oeuvre. And to fence in the imagination is even more difficult.

---

(18) D. Bax. op. cit. p. 275 ff. and *Hieronymus Bosch, his picture-writing deciphered.* Rotterdam, 1979, p. 360-9.
(19) E. H. Gombrich. «Bosch's *Garden of Delights...*» p. 162-70.

III

BOSCH'S FORMS
STYLE AND ICONOGRAPHY

If, as we have seen in the foregoing pages, Bosch's artistic training is quite unknown and that we can only assume that it elapsed in the van Akens'family workshop —on the other hand barely represented as far as preserved works are concerned— the stylistic study of our painter is studded with difficulties due to the lack of any unifying nexus between his works and his closest formal antecedents which are almost totally unknown. This sole means of hypothetical contact with other artists —his uncles, father and grandfather Jan van Aken— is perhaps the reason why Bosch is, from the stylistic point of view, what he is: a genius who was archaic in his own time. Why? On account of his isolation in his small home town of Brabant? On account of his vinculation with traditional artists? Because of his own lack of interest in solutions remote —or rather alien— to his aesthetic purposes or far removed from his intention of meaning? We have no answer to these questions but it is probable that, having analysed his work in detail, the explanation of some of the traits of his artistic praxis is to be found in these three causes. But at the same time Jeroen van Aken offers formal solutions —perhaps above all in his treatment of landscape, of his «phenomenical» vision of reality— which make him an advanced, isolated and marginal pioneer, an artist of astonishing modernity.

In a similar way to the workings of his mind, Hieronymus Bosch's technique is unique in its artistic medium and the connections which exist between his pictorial style and that of the great —and lesser— masters of Flemish «primitivism» of the 15th century are almost imaginary or, at least, insignificant. Bosch keeps on the margin of developments in painting in the southern school, Brussels, Antwerp, Bruges; far from the van Eyck's, of the Flémalle master Robert Campin, from Roger van der Weyden or from his near contemporary Hans Memling. If we turn our eyes to the north, to the Dutch or Netherland centres of the north in Haarlem and Delft —geographically nearer to Hertogenbosch—

we cannot find here either any traces of servitude or artistic dependence on Dirk Bouts, Geerten tot Sint Jans or the master of the *Virgo inter Virgines* (attributed by Panofsky to the sphere of Delft), although we may speak of certain concommittances or discoveries and solutions in common. Similarly, the search for a nexus with or roots in, the German school, with Martin Schongauer or the master E. S., would give equally negative results.

Bosch remains isolated —although not totally disconnected— and sinks his roots into the subsoil of the popular or semi-popular art of the xylographies, engravings, sculpture in wood or stone, miniature or manuscript illumination. His archaism is inspired by the eccentricities in dress of the International Gothic style of around 1400, by the fantastic mood of the marginal buffooneries of 14th century manuscripts and the irreverences of the misericords on contemporary choir stalls and, perhaps in the last instance, by the physiognomic exaggerations —coarse in their excess of reality and veracity— of the so-called *Pre-Eyckian Realism* of the south-west Netherlands. Bosch possesses all the vices and virtues of a book-illustrator yet, however, we have no information that he ever did actually work on miniatures; despite this, in all his work, the narrative element surpasses the limits of easel and panel painting, and the story portrayed is often unintelligible, as though we lacked an adjoining explanatory text of the images and as if the artist had had to resort to anti-naturalistic scrolls and graphic inscriptions to make the content clear.

If we wish to understand Bosch and understanding both him and his work means not only deciphering —as if it were a hieroglyphic— the individual symbols which recur on his panels, then we should have to enter into what Bosch, in an almost experiential way, believed in and knew; in that which made up his cultural equipment and his type of religiousness, his experience of the world and his familiarity with other artistic images; in other words, in the spirit and the art which such a spirit reflects, of his time. To achieve this, one must know at which sources our painter drank or was able to drink; not only the literary sources (we shall discuss these later), from which he was to take certain concepts or ideas and give them visual life in his work, but also the figurative sources from which he was to take certain basic artistic motifs upon which his own personality was to work in order to attain his personal oeuvre.

THE ADORATION OF THE MAGI *(frag.)*. Prado Museum, Madrid.

The figurative, iconographic, sources known by Hieronymus Bosch are another factor to be borne in mind when any analysis of his style is considered. His images and his formal treatment of them, depend on the one hand on his inimitable brush, although perhaps influenced by other forms of expression and other means of representing reality; on the other, his formal style, his configuration of images, also depends on the organization of these images in a personal manner or by following previous compositional structures, or traditional ones in scenes, stories and allegories; in other words, in iconographies. Therefore, we cannot altogether isolate the formal and iconographical field when we analyse a painter's work; the former is the ultimate expression but the latter is the subsoil, the basis on which certain forms are founded. Hence the title we have given to this chapter.

We shall attempt to develop this subject by following two different yet parallel paths and, in the last instance, two which converge. On the one hand, we shall try to offer an overall image of the formalisms and formulisms used by Bosch, of the figurative structure of his works, of the method and methods used by our painter to portray the natural reality or visionary irreality of which his paintings consist, although we shall point out existing modifications and evolutions. That is, we shall attempt a morphology of his work. On the other hand, we shall try to give a time sequence for Bosch's style despite the fact that, as his work has no unanimously accepted chronology among critics, this might be an arduous task. Along the route of this journey through his work, we shall point out the stylistic changes and novelties introduced with the passing of time, and will stress his possible formal, figurative and iconographic sources.

As Charles De Tolnay has written (1), Hieronymus Bosch's technique and style are not the result of the evolution of the school tradition, which was taken over and personally developed by him, neither was it the result of taking over an alien technique. His style and technique are the direct and adequate expression of his vision of reality, of his own particular *Weltanschauung,* which gives rise to an artistic phenomenon that had not been repeated since Jan van Eyck. Jan van Eyck painted the *totality* of the world; under the influence of late medieval Pantheism, he offered in his paintings the work of Divine Creation through Nature, as a *natura naturata.* To this end, the mythical inventor of oil painting developed his own

(1) Charles De Tolnay. *Hieronymus Bosch* (1965).–p. 45.

THE ADORATION OF THE MAGI. Prado Museum, Madrid.

style and technique which were to make his works «cosmic jewels». His equilibrium between the general and the particular (with a brush-stroke technique which makes the number of its details almost infinite, keeping at one and the same time both a microscopic and telescopic vision of reality); his figures situated in «crystallized» spaces in perfect reconstruction; the insensibilization of his characters, whose corporeity almost turns them into «objects»; his identical treatment of everything (men, fauna, flora, things, etc.), perfectly inserted into a naturally or supernaturally lit space; his symbolism which makes everything transcend its own material and physical reality; all these are the resources which Jan van Eyck placed at the service of his vision of the personal, objective and transcendent world.

Bosch, on the other hand, approached a world rejected by its metaphysical origin and which had been denied any immanent significance, and in order to portray this world, he invented a new, different type of image. The world is merely an optical illusion, a mirage of reality; clarity of vision is swathed in a mist, the inconstant substitutes the permanent, the tangible becomes the immaterial. Bosch abandons the objective description of things and his representations are the result of his particular vision of reality. But at the same time, Bosch does not only handle objective realities but also irrealities, supernatural realities which he must present in a real way; that is to say, similar in their phenomenical aspect to that of other natural objects. It is, perhaps, through this double contrary process of «making real» the irreal and «de-realizing» the real that Bosch's monsters and symbolic forms are presented to us with a materiality, formal precision and perfection perhaps greater than those of natural reality, and they become nearer to us and more «accessible»

Thus, his painting is at one and the same time *alla prima,* light and spontaneous, full of nervous expressivity, founded on a flowing and urgent, a precise and meticulously detailed script. To his taste for fluency of execution there is added his tendency to detail and precious, fine description; the solid, enamelled matter of the forms of the primitive Flemish artists is kept and reflects the refinement and draughtsman-like subtleties even in those objects of the most tenuous and ephimeral consistency and appearance; but this is a matter which, when considered in its ensemble, «from afar», becomes de-materialized. Bosch's greatest achievement is based on the fact that formal certainty, the firmness of his contours and the splendour of his colours, his immediately and instantaneously apprehensible images lend to the symbolic image an extraordinary presence of phenomenical reality and link the different outlandish episodes which fill up the space of his paintings, in visual unity; a visual unity full of power, strength and ambiguity but which, at the same time, causes them to be submerged in a subjective, irreal, fantastic environment (spacial, luminous and colouristic), which has never been experienced and which is not even practicable.

Jeroen van Aken's human figures always resemble each other, they are presented in a uniform manner as indiscriminate members of the human race rather than as individual, personal, inimitable, beings; some critics have even spoken of formal mannerism in this context. His figures seem to be as far removed from the painter's interest as they are from his eyes, they are viewed from a distance (except in the works of his last period, such as the *Epiphany* in the Prado Puseum or his later scenes from the *Passion of Christ* in Gent, London, El Escorial or Princeton), almost impassive and insensitive. On account of their minimal dimension with regard to the whole of his panels, their scant physical «weight», their lack of density and material corporeity, their almost cubic volumes, their schematism and their suppression of individualizing details, they appear indifferent to him; Bosch never tries to produce an illusion of the corporal reality through a study of their models. In his compositions, the human form only has value as an expressive contour for an anonymous subject or as a link in the narrative chain, the patient protagonist of each one of the scenes from his paintings or between the scenes themselves. As in the work of a medallist, his figures are slim, almost transparent, flattened against the surface of the panel; the chief figures are presented in decoratively attractive silhouettes lacking the heavy corporeity and sculpturesque dense with which other Flemish painters of the 15th century invested them, thanks to an intense study of Nature and careful modelling, so that it has been said that the figures of some of these painters «would displace mass, like three-dimensional bodies, if they were submerged in liquid».

The drawing and the modelling —with the light so directed as to create pronounced shading— therefore plays a secondary role in the painting of the master of Hertogenbosch. Its essentially pictorial character is based chiefly on an appropriate distribution and correct gradation of the diffuse luminosity through colour and therefore, his figures lack those tactile properties common to the early Flemish masters. It is curious to note that only in his last period, that of the large figures, Bosch resorts to broken, angular folds in the draperies of his figures, which is typical of the Netherlands school, an already traditional formula which allows him to heighten the chiaroscuro of the covered bodies and, although the anatomy thus veiled is never viewed, he manages thus to reinforce the corporeal and three-dimensional effect of his figures, but more as supports for «sculpturesque» clothes than as tangible figures beneath them. Even his grisailles are no longer true grisailles in the traditional sense of the the word in Flemish painting of the 15th century. According to the fashion started by the master of Flémalle and Jan van Eyck, the outsides of the side panels of a triptych or polyptych were decorated with paintings of images treated as if they were statues, exclusively in chiaroscuro, whites, greys and blacks; that is to say, they represented human figures as if they were monochrome stone statues, on which the light struck, thus violently showing up their volumes and mass. Jeroen van Aken rejects this way of conceiving of grisailles. In his work, except in the *Vienna Triptych,* the isolated figures have become scenes which are just as much part of the narrative as those on the inside of the panels; they are treated in monochrome but are totally lacking in their traditional sculpturesque sense although, as in the *Epiphany* of the Prado Museum, they are represented by a little sculptorial altar with an altar-piece. Polychrome figures of the donors are even inserted in the general mochrome, and are elements which break the sculptorial effect of the representation even further. Bosch's scenes on the outer panels take on the aspect of fantasmagoric narrations, in some cases totally irreal. In other triptyches, such as the *Haycart* in the Prado Museum, the outer grisaille is substituted by a totally polychrome vision, which is obviously pictorial and altogether sculptorial. In the triptych of *The Last Judgement* in the Vienna Academy, the grisailles are nearer to the traditional type. In the lower part are two semicircular arches, with fleurons and flamboyant Gothic tracery, which contain a heraldic coat of arms each. They are treated as part of real architecture, in a similar way to that used by Jan van Eyck to take in the donors and St. John's in the altarpiece of the *Adoration of the Mystic Lamb* in St. Bavon's church in Gent. However, these arches are not surrogates for a frame nor do they perform the function of diaphragm arches which separate real space from the fictitious space of the niches in which the sculptures are placed together with the polychrome praying figures of the master of Masseyck. On the other hand, in the *St. James and St. Bavon* in Vienna, in a different and contradictory way, they are framed by a landscape and an arch which leads into a room and are viewed even from different angles; thus the lack of spacial coherence is total and is underlined by the outside and in-

side of one and another scene and by the lack of relation between both figures, which do not even hold any visual or animic contact with each other. Besides, the monochrome figures are not statues; they are not raised on podiums or pedestals but live in space, move, express timidly manifested emotions. The grisaille loses all its «raison d'être» and is only maintained as a formulaic trait, a convention imposed by an established tradition. Only in the *Virgin with Child* and *St. John the Evangelist* in St. John's cathedral at Hertogenbosch do we find, in the guise of the above-mentioned clock, two true grisailles with the figures as «pictorial» sculptures on pedestals, each protected by architectonic canopies as if they were real stone statues or three-dimensional figures transferred onto canvas.

All Bosch's figures, despite the individualizing taste of the early Flemish masters and their generalized «portraiture», belong to the category of *«types»* or *ideal figures.* They lack individuality, they are not unique personages; rather, they represent generalizations, and suppress any discriminatory personal character of human types, thus converted into topical figures of different estates, paradigmatic animic attitudes or vital situations which are more circumstantial than personal. Not even the precise treatment of the anatomy of his figures seems to particularly interest Hieronymus Bosch, whether in static positions or in movement. His Eve of the *Garden of Delights,* to give an example, is kneeling in the «air» without her limbs even touching the green grass or without there being muscles under her skin. The St. James of the *Triptych of the Last Judgement* in Vienna advances in an attitude which is schematically more cautious than weary; his right foot touches the ground on trembling toes but the beating of his wings —which displays both en animic fear and lack of confidence— is more expressive than a naturalistic representation of a corporeal body which supports the weight of the pilgrim saint. His figures —so often nude— do not even appear to be organic unities but —with a slight exaggeration— unions of limbs «in a solution of continuity»; some of their necks (like those of Saint Agnes and the female donors of the Madrid *Epiphany)* painfully overlap the head and bust of their owners, as if they were cylinders stuck between two alien parts.

This lack of interest of Jeroen van Aken's for the individual was to lead to a total indifference to portrait painting. Bosch was never a portrait painter and no individual portrait —as an independent genre— has come down to us if he ever painted any. We only preserve a few portraits of donors done by him from the one in *The Marriage of Canaan* in Rotterdam to

SAINT JAMES AND ST. BAVON. Akademie der Bildenden Künste, Vienna.

those of the Prado *Epiphany.* The former is shown as wrapped in himself, hardly identifiable as a personage «on the margin» of the scene, precariously individualized in the only physiognomical features portrayed. These features are nearer to those of a specific individual than the Wise Men themselves (although there is little difference between Saint Agnes and Agnes Bosshyuise). The donors, spiritually remote as portraits (a fact which is intensified when they are framed within a scene or landscape), are far removed from the spectator, somewhat «generalized», too, stressed more in their uniqueness of what they have in common with the rest of humanity, almost typified as generic donors. There are no autonomous personalities which strike us with their physical or animic immediacy, there are no emotions, only impersonal presences; there is no interpretation of a personality in Bosch's portraits; there is almost not even an exact physical description of one.

But although Bosch avoids individual description and «typifies» the diverse human genres, it is logical that he should on the contrary feel atracted by those human forms in which the «typifying» features are carried to an extreme: caricatures. It is not the individual in itself which holds interest for him, but the individual in its deformity, the pure excess of generically significant individuality, the caricature. From his early youthful work on, this interest in caricature exists, as is shown by his *Two Priestly Heads* in the Boymans-van Beuningen Museum in Rotterdam, but it is accentuated above all when he portrays the priests and yearning populace in his *Ecce Homo* and *Ostentatio Christi* (Frankfurt, Boston, Philadelphia) or his *Way to Calvary* (Vienna, Royal Palace Madrid) and, even more, in those works on similar subjects which belong to his last period *(The Coronation of Thorns* in London, Prado Museum; *Christ before Pilate)* in Princeton; *The Way to Calvary in Gent;* or the not unanimously acknowledged as Bosch's originals: *Christ before Pilate* in Rotterdam and Sao Paolo (Brasil) or the *Kiss of Judas* in San Diego, (California).

The portrayal of Christ's judges, executioners, Jews, or evil-doers of diverse sorts, as horribly grotesque beings, deformed in their originally human features, physically «animalized» on account of their perversions, was already an old practice and good examples of it may be found in typical works of so-called Pre-Eyckian realism. Perhaps Bosch's caricatures of his younger and mature periods are in the same traditional line but the judges of his last period (above all those in Princeton and Bruges) surpass the limits established by their predecessors and by his own work prior to this. The secondary characters of these two paintings, with their features markedly accentuated and their faces reduced to animal masks, has given rise to the idea of the possible influence of Leonardo da Vinci's caricatures; Bosch would have known these latter thanks to his hypothetical trip to Italy or otherwise through prints. In the first place, however, one may argue against this influence on the strength of the previous existence of less elaborate caricatures —less exaggerated ones— in the master of Hertogenbosch's own paintings and in Flemish and German popular tradition still alive at the time. On the other hand, Leonardo's caricatures are more pure caricatures in the normal sense of the word, studies —one might almost say scientific ones— of physiognomy (2); research on man from animal models, as if the facial features of some men were built upon the underlying animal structures. In Bosch, on the contrary, they are true human caricatures, which take up elements from the animal world like footnotes, in search of an expressive accentuation of certain moral qualities which, because of their depravity and bestiality, tend to resemble those of the fiercest or basest animals in their outer features.

For Jeroen van Aken, Christs' judges are deshumanized representations of Evil, expressive forms which are accentuated when they are frequently placed in pure profile. There is expressionism here and not exaggerated researching into human gestural modes and we should bear in mind that Leonardo da Vinci defined *decorum* or mode as the property of the gestures, dress and place of the characters in a scene. Gesture, as a primordial part of human configuration, should respond perfectly to the social and moral characteristics and qualities of a personage; gestures could modify facial features in a specific way and this would lead to the obvious characterization of an individual in a painting, but without the character's losing his human properties for this reason. In this without the character's losing his human properties for this reason. In this sense, the difference which exists between two works of Bosch's near contemporary Quentin Massys (1465/6-1530), is illuminating: these works are his *Old Knight* in the Macquemart-André Museum, Paris (dated 1513) and his *Ugly Duchess* in the London National Gallery. In the former, there is a caricature, one might say in the Italian Style; in the latter there is a

(2) Ernst H. Gombrich. «The Grotesque Heads» in *The Heritage of Apelles. Studies in the Art of the Renaissance*. London 1976. p. 57 ff.

remodelling rather than a deformation, of the facial reality of the old lady portrayed, with a marked intention of expressing certain moral qualities. Yet, however, Massys does not go as far as to animalize his model's features. Bosch's caricatures are, if one may say so, «second degree» caricatures, remodellings (from other models) of certain deformations of human features, caricatures of other caricatures for the sake of greater expressivity.

In Bosch's work, man co-exists with other beings, animals and objects. Jeroen van Aken's style, by using the same more pictorial than sculptural technique, attains a higher degree of naturalism and reality in the non-human, an effect of the immediate presence of the object or thing viewed and contemplated by the spectator. If the animals of each of the different species may still be considered as archetypes, the same is not true of other realities, above all those in which their presence has greater symbolic value and the nature of which is farther removed from everyday reality. These animals, symbolic objects or mosters, appear to us not only as «types», but with a profoundly stressed individualization, almost with a quality of uniqueness. They have not only presence as visual forms, contours without weight or any other physical qualities, but they show themselves to the spectator as the vehicles of other properties. They have tactile, volumentric, massive presence; their surfaces display material qualities hitherto unsuspected; they are hard or soft objects, solid or fragile, smooth or rough, rigid or flexible, fleshy or boney, crystalline or mineral, vegetable or animal. Their real or imaginary nature, by means of finer detail and more careful and meticulous modelling, are offered to us in all their visual and material value. Bosch achieves a high degree of virtuosism in these elements, perhaps above all in his representation of hard, brittle objects such as the fantastic naturalistic architecture of *The Garden of Delights.* One might say that Bosch insists on the naturalistic representation of the non-real, which needs far greater tangible support than that required by the real, the known and experienced, the presence and existence of which is taken for granted and a knowledge of which —even though it may go through a schematization process— is easy for the spectator as such. Where the real and material aspect of things should be insisted on is in those which are totally irreal.

We believe that this double treatment of the natural and the supernatural is also quite clear in the two types of symbolism used by Jeroen van Aken. We are not going to discuss here —we shall do so elsewhere—

ECCE-HOMO *(frag.)*. Stadelsches Museum, Frankfurt.

what the symbols of Bosch's paintings mean but the typology of his symbolism, of the two types which, despite their common trascendence, respond to two different types of reality: occult or disguised symbolism and direct, open or ovbious symbolism.

In medieval Christian art, to refer to the temporal and geographical sphere with which we are concerned, there always existed an obvious type of symbolism; that is to say, conventional forms which were used to substitute concepts or ideas that could not be represented because they were mental abstractions; invisible phenomena, irreal, supernatural, lacking form. Whether this meant personal attributes, personifications with attributes, symbols with formal credibility with regard to what they represented, or incongruent, monstrous or conventional symbols, these forms or figures were imbued with a phenomenical presence which is totally acceptable to the spectator although their function might be purely significant and not as naturalistic description. Besides, in a work of art, scenes and characters of other epochs and other places could appear, their presence being justified on the symbolic, although not on the realistic, plane. They appeared, then, outside any logical context from the point of view of a coherent representation in space and time, as allegories, premonitions, anticipations of logical conclusions, from an intellectual or religious point of view but not a visually empirical one.

In 15th century Flemisg painting, another type of symbolism, the disguised type, reaches its peak. This type of symbolism, invented by 14th century Italian painters and already practised by certain Flemish masters of the end of the 14th (such as Melchior Braederlam de Ypres, for example), responded to the increasingly wide-spread taste for coherently naturalistic representations on the whole. An art which practised the temporal and spacial unities (through logical control and perspective) and sought the natural representation of reality, was obliged to reject the intrusive open symbolism of the past (excepting perhaps certain supernatural phenomena such as miracles, visions, angels or devils which defied the laws of Nature). But what it could not abandon completely was the trascendent nature of many of the facts and representations which it had to paint. It had to find another vehicle, an apparently real one, for these meanings. The solution lay in the diguise of reality of symbolic elements, based on the Thomistic tenet that physical objects are spiritual realities in the form of corporeal metaphors.

Robert Campin, the master of Flémalle, opened up the «modern» way of disguised symbolism, although there still appeared in his works objects which were apparently devoid of symbolic significance. With Jan van Eyck, this method achieved the rank of representative system: the whole of his painted reality is saturated with meaning. Romanesque or Gothic building, in ruins or intact (as representation of the pre-Christian or Christian world), natural light (natural or supernatural according as to whether it comes from the south or north, from right or left), windows or other tripartite bays (the symbol of the Trinity), candles, fruit, lilies, glass decanters, washbasins (diverse Marian symbols of Her different sacred attributes), etc., all are presented to us as natural phenomena or objects, and at the same time, impregnated whit a specific and perfectly evident symbolism for the connaisseur of such a code then in force. Thus, the hidden symbols were kept alive throughout the 15th century (although their systematic use was sometimes lost) and they came to timidly penetrate the modern world.

However, when direct symbolism gives way to the hidden type and this latter almost totally substitutes the former, Bosch deliberately and archaically chooses the open symbols, although he does not discard the disguised ones, which were fully alive in his time. It is without a doubt that the fantastic, irreal world of Bosch (that of the *Last Judgements* to *The Garden of Delights*) could only be peopled with symbols of an obvious nature and that an out- and-out naturalism was out of place. It is also true that the hidden symbolism was used almost exclusively in scenes from Scripture (above all of the Life of the Virgin and Infancy of Christ) in which a feeling of quotidien plausibility was valued above all, a feeling of naturalness in the settings. The «images» of the Virgin, the Annunciations, the Epiphanies, etc., was the most suitable field for hidden symbolism. There are few works of this type, New Testament Scripture stories which it appears Bosch painted, but in them the disguised symbolism is on the one hand still timidly used and, on the other, it is mixed with open symbols.

In any early work such as *The Marriage of Canaan* in Rotterdam, Hieronymus Bosch presents disguised symbols (alongside open ones) in the sort of cupboard at the back or staggered altar, or in the sculptures which crown the columns of the ribbed-vaulted chapel; but in these sculptures there occurs the obviousness, the de-naturalization of the symbol disguised as a statue for one of them, taking on life, slips through an opening in the spandrel of the arches. The disguised symbol, when it is

THE GARDEN OF DELIGHTS *(frag.).* Prado Museum, Madrid.

de-realized, becomes a direct symbol. In the *Adoration of the Child* in Cologne, there is a notable lack of disguises. If one disregards Bosch's polemical *Epiphanies* (the Kleinberg-Johnson one in New York-Philadelphia, probably a workshop painting, that in the Matropolitan Museum of New York of doubtful authorship and the one in London possibly a copy), the three certain ones of his come to only three. The one in the Philadelphia Museum already displays one of the typical formulas of Bosch's hidden symbolism; scenes remote in time and place but connected to the chief representation as its prefigurations or allegories (in this case the *Falling of Manna in the Desert*) are painted as decoration of the costume or headdress of one of the protagonists; in this case, the little scene embroidered on the black king's sleeve may be interpreted as a prefiguration of the Last Supper, the Eucharist and the Mass, a meaning confirmed by the liturgical objects donated by the Magi (also as disguised symbols), instead of the traditional gold, frankinsense and myrrh.

In the *Adoration of the Magi* in Madrid and Anderlecht, these devices take on greater importance. In the Prado work, the outer grisaille (with the *Mass of St. Gregory* and its altar with little scenes from Christ's Passion surrounding an image of *Ecce Homo*) functions as a prefiguration of the inner Epiphany. In this latter, disguised symbols appear in the form of sculptures on a Gothic building in a state of ruin (3) or on the gifts and clothes of Melchior, Caspar and Balthasar; Even the attribute of the patron Saint Agnes, the lamb, appears in the guise of a live animal, peacefully lying on the grass at some distance from the martyr near a shepherd's crook (that of the Good Shepherd), as if it were an object forgotten by the shepherds who peep through the cabin. In the Anderlecht triptych, the same elements are displayed and as in the Madrid panel, there are symbols and direct personifications such as the disconcerting Fourth Wise King, the Antichrist or Herod in an outlandish head-dress. Likewise, scenes of an eminently narrative quality are depicted quite out of place with the iconography of the panels, but bearing allegorical significance.

The disguised symbols in Bosch's works, as we have seen, are present mainly in his Biblical pictures, which does not mean that open sym-

---

(3) Interpreted as the Palace of Solomon or David. From the point of view of post-Eyckian hidden symbolism, the use of Gothic architecture —contemporary— would be incongruent. It should be remembered that the Romanesque style (or, more traditionally, pseudo-oriental) represented, as did ruins, the pagan world, or the pre-Christian or Jewish one. On the other hand, Gothic architecture and intact buildings referred symbolically to historical Christianity.

bols or narrative-allegorical scenes are missing, as true complements to the overall meaning of the painting, which is in turn heightened and enriched by the nondisguised symbols and allegories. In this sense, and with the same aim of giving greather complexity to the scenes full of direct symbols, the disguised ones appear in other works which are markedly fantastic and anti-naturalistic. Thus, for example, in the sculpted scenes in the pseudo-Tower of Babel in the *Temptations of Saint Anthony* in Lisbon and perhaps as representations of the vision of the hermit, in the form of prefigurations of Christ's Baptism, Pentecost and the temptations themselves.

Bosch's men, animals, natural or artificial objects, more or less monstrous symbols, are both placed and move in space. De Tolnay (4) has pointed out that the impression of space in Bosch's work is produced by overlapping or superposing different colours on zones parallel to the plane of the picture and that their aesthetic gradation determines the laws of space: the darkest tones prevail in the lower parts of the work, becoming pregressively lighter in lighter zones as they approach the line of the horizon, to then darken once more in the sky. By means of this procedure, in a certain sense a pioneer representation of perspective which is know as «aerial», the artist creates an extraordinary atmospheric sensation and one of spacial depth which, however, remains characterised as visionary air and space. From this point of view, Bosch shows himself to be an original researcher in pictorial aerial perspective as against geometric, lineal perspective. Nevertheless, things do not appear to be as simple as this. It is true that Jeroen van Aken meant an advance in the conquest of a naturalistic vision of reality, but this was achieved by renouncing certain then traditional devices in order to create naturalistically unitary and homogeneous spacial effects.

The gigantic step forward taken in Italy and the Netherlands in the 15th century toward the achievement of a naturalistic representation of space, is based on perspective, on the scientific and empiric discovery, respectively, of a method which would permit the constant reduction of objects placed at an ever increasing distance from the artist's and spectator's point of view. Perspective, in the first place, as a representative method, allowed the artist to reduce the size of things seen at a greater distance; secondly, it supplied a method for the construction of the su-

---

(4) De Tolnay. *op. cit.* p. 45.

rrounds of that space —landscape or exterior, architectonic or interior— in such a way that its representation coincided with our visual experience of that space. Lineal, geometric perspective in the modern sense, is only one of the aspects of the general concept of perspective.

The modern method of perspective —based on Brunellsch and Eyck to give the names of some pioneer artists— as against other less perfect attempts which we shall mention later, lies in the organization of space from a unique, fixed point of view and, as its reflection in the horizon, from a unique disappearing point. The correct construction, according to this method, means that all parallel lines (without taking into account their situation or direction) converge in one of the possible infinite disappearing points and that all orthogonal lines (parallel perpendicular to the plane of the picture) converge in a unique, central disappearing point, definable as the point of the infinite on which the spectator's or artist's point of view is projected and which determines the horizon of the picture. The line of the horizon is the zone in which all the disappearing points of all the parallels in the picture are situated, and which are organized on horizontal planes. All equal sizes diminish in direct proportion to their distance from the eye of the spectator and the viewpoint «of the picture».

This method, which meant the modern conception of space as three-dimensional, continuous and infinite, allowed the artist to clarify the size and relative position of corporeal objects in space represented through painting and to organize the limits of that space —floors, ceilings, walls— in a coherent manner. As from the second half of the 15th century, above all in Italy and Flanders, the monofocal system of perspective was common practice to all progressive artists or, at least, to all those who were concerned with a naturalistic type of painting, whether Flemish primitive or Italian renaissance. Did Jeroen van Aken, alias Bosch, form part of this group?

In the first place, Bosch diminishes the size of identical figures according to the distance at which they are placed in relation to the spectator but their reduction does not follow the rule established by the laws of modern perspective, but the dictates of his own visual experience, without any «scientific» support. Let us examine a clarifying example. In the *Paradise* of the left wing of the *Haycart* triptych, we find Adam and Eve portrayed three times, in three scenes which are placed in the Garden of

THE WAY TO CALVARY *(frag.).* Royal Palace, Madrid.

Eden but which correspond to three different-episodes of their lives, separated by time in reality and united in the fiction of the painting: the creation of Eve appears in the last instance, in the middle of the temptation, in the foreground the Expulsion from Paradise. A painter such as Dirk Bouts (one should remember his panels of the *Justice of the Emperor Oton III*) used this device, dictated by the narrative sense of the subject portrayed, but he had given a coherent aspect to space and figures portrayed therein by means of a progressive reduction of the sizes of these figures according as to whether they were nearer to or further from the foreground of the picture. In the Madrid *Paradise*, Bosch reduces his figures of our forefathers, but not in a progressive way determined by their placing within the landscape space of his panel. Adam and Eve expelled from Paradise are larger than those tempted by the Serpent and these latter are larger than Adam asleep and Eve being born, but the difference in size is greater between these latter and the temptation figures than that between these latter and those expelled when the distance between the fore- and middle ground is much larger than that between the middle and background. In other pictures by Boch this type of problem is solved by identical means: progressive reduction, but one which is neither continuous nor coherent and systematic as far as distance is concerned.

On the other hand, Jeroen van Aken ignores the naturalistic dimensional relationships between figures, objects and surrounding buildings, even in pictures which are not fantastic and in which objects and buildings could lose their true dimensions in favour of greater expressive power. The characters (from those of the little scenes in the early panel of the *Seven Deadly Sins* to those of the late *Epiphany* in the Prado) are too large in relation to the buildings which act as background to them or else these latter are too small to accomodate the figures comfortably. In the *Epiphany* in the Prado Museum, if the seated Virgin stood up, she would smash the ceiling of the «stall», thus causing new holes in its structure, which would then be immediately used by the curious shepherds as peepholes to watch the scene through. In certain cases, such as in *Envy* of the Madrid table, or in the *Paradise*, his architectonic structures bring to mind the so-called «dolls'-house architecture» (5) of Italian 14th century painting and that of the Franco-Flemish painters of around

---

(5) Erwin Panofsky. *Renacimiento y renacimientos en el arte occidental.* Madrid, 1975. Chap. 3 and *La perspectiva como forma simbólica,* Barcelona, 1973.

1400, which is viewed from outside and within and is of an unbelievable size for the figures it contains.

Bosch's interior views are also illustrative of his disregard for the unitary reproduction of space or of his poor handling of devices which were already traditional during his lifetime. If at any time van Aken was concerned with scenes taking place within an architectonic interior, this was during his youthful period for later there is a remarkable absence of such scenes. The episodes with interiors of the *Table* (*Extreme Unction, Pride, Sloth, Gluttony*) are portrayed framed in badly constructed rooms, in which the orthogonal lines do not converge in a unique disappearing point or in which the planes, which should, in theory be parallel to one another (floors and the seats of stools and chairs, the boards of tables), do not converge in the infinite when prolonged, but long before; different points of view cross each other for different objects, there is no spacial unity whatsoever. In the *Marriage of Canaan* the same thing occurs. Even *The Miser's Death* in Washington, apparently the best constructed architectonic interior in Bosch's work, suffers similar faults. The orthogonal lines do not converge in a unique disappearing point but in a series of them placed on a vertical line; that is, almost in a perspective construction based on the plurifocal «fish-bone» method or in a «disappearing area» of likewise 14th century origin. On the other hand, the interiors are reproduced from a very high viewpoint (which reminds one of those used in contemporary urban cartography in *mounted* perspective), almost «birds-eye views». This high viewpoint stops the spectator from feeling «within» the picture or within the scene painted; the interior is alien to us in its spaciality and is quite independent; the fictitious aspect of the picture is not a prolongation of the spectator's real space; we never get the feeling of having penetrated on our own feet into the interiors and of having lived side-by-side with the characters of the scene. In this as in other matters, Bosch kept out of the innovating currents of his time.

Neither in this sense does Bosch make use of one of the then common devices used to create space round an object: shading. Not all the objects in one same scene project shade and when they do produce shade, they often do so in a totally asystematic way, without responding to the direction of the main focus of light nor being graded according to the existance of secondary focuses. If in Bosch there is no rigurous spacial construction, neither does he display any rigorous regulation of light and illumination, tending to a diffuse and imprecise luminosity.

It is also interesting to note another type of «spacial device» used by van Aken: the negation of space. In some of his pictures (*Ecce Homo* in Frankfurt, Boston and Philadelphia, for example) the masses of characters and judges destroy the space in which they should be situated, some being heaped on top of others in an irreal conglomeration. In others (scenes from the *Paradise* in London, Madrid, Princeton or Ghent, of the last period), space is denied more directly: it exists neither among the figures nor around the compact human forms. In one case (*The Crowning of Thorns* in El Escorial) the real, open background has been discarded; the background is blocked by a golden «wall» which acts as a background curtain. This archaic device was originally meant in painting to lend the work a decorative aspect to illustrate material richness, the value of which was transferred to the subject of the picture. Roger van der Weyden had used it in his *Descent from the Cross* in the Prado Museum, with the aim of not distracting the spectator's attention by using a figurative landscape background and thus concentrating the inner passion of the scene to the utmost. In his *Crucifixions* in the Pennsylvania Museum of Art or El Escorial, he had worked in a similar way, substituting the golden background for a smooth wall covered by hanging drapery. In the case of Bosch, one should think that this device is due to the same objective of intensifying the drama represented in view of his next step in search of such an intensification, which was not to be the blocking out of space but by means of its negation as a three-dimensional, continuous and infinite substance.

In his *Christ Before Pilate,* and above all, in his *Way to Calvary* in Ghent, Hieronymus Bosch disregards the qualities of continuity and infinitude of space. The figures —busts or heads— are crowded together and block space out of their surroundings; space is formed by their jostling bodies; beyond them space practically does not exist. In a composition which is presided by the principle of the *horror vacui* or horror of the void, the characters become the background to the scene; the background is no longer neutral to intensify the protagonists' expressions, the background is expressive in itself insofar as it has absorbed the protagonists themselves from the scene, in a scene in which all the characters are foreground, middle-ground and background, surface and distance —without any space between one and another— of the picture.

It is however, in the landscape space that Bosch was to place all his interest, far more so than in the interior space of his youthful period or in the spacial negation of his final works. His interest in landscape as a backdrop and frame in which his scenes take place is enormous and the results are highly attractive. His wide, detailed landscapes are viewed by the painter from a position far above ground-level; they break with composition on a *plateau* (6), in «plain or tableland» (in which the figures are placed on the ground but are outlined against the sky), typical of primitive Flemish painting of the most innovating type, and raise the viewpoints and disappearing points of the spectator and picture enormously. To this effect, the horizon is raised almost to the top part of his panels and allows us to contemplate a wide extension of ground, with a suitable space to scatter his little figures and secondary scenes. The sky is kept high up, not as a background, and the figures are placed on the ground. They do not dominate the landscape from a protagonist's position, but are immersed in it. On the other hand and despite this very high viewpoint, the figures —not even those which are in the foreground— have not undergone any perspective deformation whatsoever (looking from top to bottom) neither have they been foreshortened. The vertical plane of the picture is visually very far from the spectator and this latter is left outside the fictitious space of the painting. A true illusion of depth or spacial reality cannot come nor does it come, from a dualism in the construction of the perspective. The plane of the ground, which is too steep, comes back at the spectator and is almost confused with a background in the form of a landscape backcloth.

All the planes, terms, of the environment painted display the same clarity and perfection of detail, even the farthest away. Bosch is not interested in the ethos of his compositions except as one more element of that expressive reality which he so personally conforms and deforms at one and the same time both in a realistic and visionary way. The landscape is immersed —in its mineral and vegetable structure— in the whole of the meaning. Like Bosch's figures, it is an element which, on account of its tangible visual reality, draws us towards his world peopled with ambiguity, extravagance and mystery.

However, Bosch's landscapes display a strange degree of unity. The parallel between the colour zones which the painter superposes on the

(6) Millard Meiss. «Jan van Eyck and the Italian Renaissance» and *«Highlands»* in Lowlands: Jan van Eyck, the Master of Flémalle and the Franco-Italian Tradition» in *The Painter's Choice. Problems in the Interpretation of Renaissance Art.* New York, 1976. Chaps. 2 and 3. This latter previously in *Gazette des Beaux-Arts,* LVII, 1961. p. 273-314.

panel lends this impression of unity to his environments, rather visually than spacially coherent. His style, based more on colour than on line, produces the effect of a rare dematerializad and visionary reality, almost like a mirage that would disappear as if by magic should the thresholds of his pictures and their fictitious spaces be tresspassed. To this end, there is no foreground in his works with small figures. In those with large figures of his last period, the colour foregrounds are made up either of the flat silhouette of the figures or else by a single figure which forms a unity with the whole of the foreground. The middle-grounds disappear and the figures show up directly against the background.

The unity of landscape in Bosch is thus proportionate through his use of colour and therefore it has been said that he took part in the discovery (maybe in an unconscious way) of aerial perspective. This is a later method in the process of conquering the naturalistic representation of environmental reality, but Jeroen van Aken dematerializes («aerializes») his landscapes in search of expressiveness and not of fidelity to the reality reflected by the phenomenon of sight. This is more obvious in his best landscapes, perhaps the farthest removed from the canons of primitive Flemish painting. Close to these latter one may set those of the *Epiphany* in the Prado or those of *St. Christopher* in Rotterdam and the *St. John the Baptist* in the Madrid Lázaro-Galdiano Museum. As opposed to these paintings, there are other landscapes in which the visionary and dematerialized aspect is accentuated. One should bear in mind the infernal depths of the *Garden of Delights,* in the environments of *Visions of the Hereafter* in Venice, of the *Temptations of St. Anthony* in Lisbon, or more than anything, in the phantasmagoric landscapes of the *Triptych of the Flood* in Rotterdam.

In these paintings, the illumination and lighting, the air and smoke become at one and the same time both palpable and fantastic by means of a meticulously perfected treatment of colour. The effect of *Stimmung* (7) is accentuated, as likewise that of visual harmony, of a continued atmosphere which perhaps makes one think of Bosch's dependence on the work of Dirk Bouts or Geerten tot Sint Jans. This atmospheric feeling, besides the special use of colour, also makes use of formulas which intensify it: the violent back lighting of planes and matte objects (the buildings of the *Garden* or the *Haycart)* or the «over-exposition» to light as in

---

(7) E. Panofsky. Early..., p. 318-9.

CHRIST BEFORE PILATE. The Art Museum, Princeton.

an overexposed photograph (the forest of the *Temptations* in Lisbon), for example. There is also monochromy along the lines of traditional landscape, such as in the *Prodigal Son* in Rotterdam, which accentuates the environmental coherence and unity by essentially pictorial devices and that of animic *resonance* by means of a principally expressive objective. This emotional *consonance* is heightened even further in his *Triptych of the Flood* (or in the grisaille of the world after the Flood, that of the supposedly *Antediluvian World* of the *Garden of Delights*); the almost total monochromy and the treatment of colour as if it were almost gouache or wash arouse in the spectator a feeling of desolation, sadness, the dense, oppressive environmental unity being only comparable to those produced by some of Rembrandt's etchings or certain *Proverbs* and *Follies* of Goya's done in acquatint.

This is one of Bosch's greatest achievements in the use of colour schemes, that is, his intensification of the sense of homogeneity, which even manages to give body and atmosphere to his most visionary scenes. Bosch's colours, as De Tolnay has written, do not portray the actual substance of the objects or their textures, but fundamentally express a varied substance which is uniquely specific of the colours themselves. The artist's negative attitude towards naturalistic fidelity leads him to an irrational play of irridescent tones, of violent colour contrasts or tenuous modulations on grisaille. Light, through colour, heightens the «lack of substance» of this type of painting.

We have already said that the light of Hieronymus Bosch's paintings is predominatly diffuse. Jeroen van Aken covers his figures and objects in the foreground with a white or pink patina of more intense light which contrasts at times with his landscape backgrounds. In his last works Bosch uses a tenuous chiaroscuro and almost transparent shading. «The artist substitutes individualized representation of things for the direct representation of a global vision which, based on his knowledge, modulates and enriches» (8). Bosch begins his works with a white layer on which he sketches his composition in with black stone. Over this sketch he spreads a thin layer of pale beige colour on which the final painting is carried out with fine brushes and transparent oil colours. If other primitive Flemish painters had achieved a type of painting which reminds one of the colour effects of enamelling on the strength of the

---

(8) De Tolnay. *op. cit.* p. 46-47.

THE SHIP OF FOOLS. The Louvre, Paris.

superposition of translucent glazes over more or less opaque under-layers, a technique which was characterized by its shine and deep lights (either internal or in depth and not merely superficial) and its brilliance of colour, with this technique the colour effects of the printing layers disappeared, the light and colour contrasts were heightened and, at another, aesthetic level, they managed to express the essentially static nature of reality in an appropiate way. Hieronymus Bosch's technique, on the other hand, which was transparent, supple and continuous, became the ideal means of representing his idea of reality as being in a state of disintegration. This same type of technique was to be practised with identical intentions, in his drawings.

In those of his drawings which have been preserved, Jeroen van Aken displays a new technical advance. The primitive Flemish artists had mainly used a silver point, a means by which they had achieved linear designs in which sculptorial effects and the shading was done in lines. Those artist who used a pen did so following the rules laid down by the technique of fine silver point and the effects thus derived were almost identical. Bosch rejects the silver point and almost exclusively uses pen, albeit with other formal, expressive intentions, which become more and more manifest as his career progresses. At the beginning, his drawings are still too linear and are constructed on the basis of straight lines; later they tend to bring in a calligraphy full of flamboyant curves; at the end of his life, his drawing is simplified and is organized on the strength of synthetic lines and small strokes which incorporate certain hitherto unachieved pictorial effects into a yet essentially linear technique, by pressing harder or softer on the pen-nib thus leaving streaks of different width and intensity of colour.

With such formal means and structural schemata and formulas, as we have just discussed, Bosch naturally achieves compositions of a highly personal nature. We shall see later the influence of other artists' compositions on van Aken and the modifications and variations introduced by him based on inherited compositional lay-outs, or his particular iconograms based on traditional iconographies. His early compositions keep to the simplest of lay-outs, flimsily ordered on geometric patterns of great simplicity, most of which are rhomboidal (The Marriage of Canaan, the Epiphany of Philadelphia, the Ecce Homo in Frankfurt, etc.) and which are appropriately adapted to the spacial organization of his pictures. In this sense, Bosch often uses architectonic or furniture structures which help to visually define such compositional lay-outs.

In the works of his central period, that of his maturity, the compositions are constructed from simple juxtaposed horizontal planes, from bottom to top, with elements of organic union between them and which discard any apriorism which may bring in ordering or regulating overall geometric designs. Bosch is fond of a type of organization, similar to that in tapestries, which resembles a theatrical scenographic distribution, the proscenium arch being kept for the secondary episodes or those which allude to the main one; the front stage becomes the centre of attraction; the sloping background is kept for producing the environmental effect where his landscapes unfold themselves, full of small significant figures. Sometimes, the various scenes scattered over the different planes of the work display unifying features between each other which follow a zig-zag lay-out as if it were likewise a landscape series of soft hills or streams which overlap on their banks and flow in broken meanders across the plains. At other times there may be seen in the central parts of his paintings geometric, elliptical or semi-elliptical organizations which order several scenes into a wide curve (as the primitive Femish painters did in their general compositions), like actors on a stage.

In his last period, Bosch returns to rhomboidal compositions for his paintings with large figures for the foregrounds, and still uses the juxtaposition or superposition of planes for the background, which are connected to each other by the above-mentioned zig-zag strokes. But he also introduces a completely new compositional device. His Biblical paintings based on half figures have insistently drawn attention not only on account of their spacial denial and their *horror vacui* which we have already discussed, but also for the appearance of half-figure characters in them. The coincidences of this type of composition with those of the Venetians at the end of the *Quattrocento* have already been pointed out, from Giambellino to the young Titian. The thesis which supports Hieronymus Bosch's trip to Italy may find in these characteristics one more formal proof to back up its arguments. However, there is no need to go so far afield; half-figures within a Flemish artistic context are numerous in portraits and in the type of the *Virgin and Child* by Roger van der Weyden which is of half-figures and which was widely spread by his followers and imitators and was taken over into other iconographies such as the *Descent from the Cross.* In fact, Bosch may well have followed this type of *Madonna* for his *Adoration of the Child* in Cologne or may have reached it through the Suppression of the lower half of pictures devoted to penitent saints kneeling before an altar, table or rock. The existence of this type of «supports» for the lower half of a figure's body may have led an artist

to take out the lower half and use the support as the basis of his con-
centrated composition. It might be significant of this intensifying reduction that Bosch's first work with a half-figure may have been a penitent or tempted *St. Anthony,* today missing but known through two
copies with variants, one in the Ansterdam Rijksmuseum and the other in
the Madrid Prado Museum (9).

From what we might call an aesthetic viewpoint, we see how Bosch
does not pay much attention to problems of the compositional type, a
fact which seems rather archaic than original or innovating in his compositional system. If his environmental and atmospheric unity sought animic
expression and his symbolic structure the expression of a moral content,
his compositions are simplified in their tendency to facilitate a reading of
the story told in the picture. The composition is justified by the narrative
structure of Bosch's works.

It seems doubtless that the didactic and moralizing intentions of Hieronymus Bosch's works favoured their development as edifying narrati-
ves, as «stories» (sometimes divided in different «strips»), illustrations of
didactic texts which held some continuous and univerally valid moral.
The compositional structure of his works (as from the table of the *Seven
Deadly Sins)* and their diverse scondary scenes which complete the overall meaning of his «pictures» are to this end abounding, thus collabora-
ting in the clear transmission of a message. Even the narrative nature,
rather illustrative than the introduction of «images», seems to be underlined by the apparition, above all in his youthful period, of explicative captions, which facilitate and complete a reading of the image rather like the
text at the bottom of a photograph.

We shall attempt to go into this aspect of Bosch's work in depth by
analyzing his personal narrative and illustrative formulas according to
the different types of works. From the thematic point of view, Hieronymus
Bosch's work may be divided into four large groups: scenes from the life
of Christ (basically from the Passion), his pictures of saints, his visions
of man's ultimate destiny, and lastly, his works of a more exclusive and
purely allegorical or moral nature.

---

(9) There are, however, critics who consider those works to be imitations of the master's style instead of copies of a lost original or Bosch's.

CROSSBOWMAN. Prado Museum, Madrid.

Within the first group, Bosch does not only attempt to show a historical event —*hic et nunc*— from the life of Christ but displays the universal and permanent implications and connotations which may be derived from this event. This intention is already present in one of his earliest works such as *The Marriage of Cannan;* in this work, the enological miracle is first tranformed into a premonition of universal validity of the sacramental eucharist, the miracle which continually occurs whenever the priest pronounces the words of consecration; at the same time Bosch lends a note of actuality to the evangelical theme by disguising it in an almost popular generic scene in its precision. The representatione and his sense of actualization are heightened because he allows the spectator to identify with what is happening in the banquet scene, and underlines this possibility by the appearance of the two peeping-toms at the back of the picture, with whom the spectator may mentally exchange places.

This presence of spectators in the scenes within a picture is a device used profusely by the painter, from his youthful *Epiphany* in Philadelphia to the later one in the Prado. The profusion of judges in vociferating, hostile crowds in his scenes from the Passion like film «extras» or theatre supernumeraries may also have this same meaning. On occasions they attain almost protagonist status which inverts the traditional meaning of iconography. The judges become the main characters of the drama (the spectators) and Christ disappears as a *historical* personage. This dehistorization of the scenes from the Passion is heightened by ridiculing —by means of deforming caricature— the representatives of sin and Evil and by thus depriving the historical event of «seriousness». Bosch in this also echoes an ancient tradition in medieval didactic poetry which did not portray the devil and evil as against God and Good in an antagonic, dramatic conflict, to a certain extent invested with dignity as in ancient psychomachies, but ridiculed them.

In these pictures of the Passion the master of Hertogenbosch often introduces different secondary scenes (most of these are perhaps to be found in the grisailles of the Lisbon *Triptych),* which, occurring successively in the evangelical story or being personal additions put in by the artist, are offered to us in a visually «synchronic» form whilst their detailed reading requires a «diachronic» itinerary through the diverse zones of the picture. In these works, the narrative nature leads the painter to include several successive scenes from evangelical history; thus, surely the *Ecce Homo* or *Ostentatio Christi* in Philadelphia is a secondary frag-

THE CONCERT OF THE EGG. Palais des Beaux-Arts, Lille.

ment of a larger composition now missing, which would have had as its main subject a *Way to Calvary.*

Thus these pictures on Biblical themes are offered to us as moralizing premonitions or allegories rather than images, «histories» of a sacred historical event, or as «tales» or stories with a moral which may be applied to all spectators to a certain extent, and not as «icons», or reverential images worthy of iconolatry. In exactly the same way as with his images of saints, not even his *Ecce Homo* or *Ostentatio Christi* —one of the most purely assimilable iconographies within sacred icons— are portrayed as sacred images but as moral narrations.

Likewise, Bosch's saints are portrayed as examples of moral life but not as mute icons, abstract in their message. These saints are also portrayed in scenes from their lives, in hagiographic typology, the saints appear immersed in the world —from which they attempt to isolate themselves or which perturbs them—. It tempts and disconcerts them, it is a world that is ever present. This worldly presence —almost invariably seen through a negative prism— is specified through symbols or episodes of an anechdotic nature (fires, deaths, disasters)which reinforce the sense of «present» in his works. Their narrative nature is heightened by means of these devices and reaches its climax in the temptations visualised in different scenes —real or imagined by the saint— which minutely illustrate the diverse types of sinful worldly attractions which surround us. In the *St. Anthony* of Lisbon, three scenes from the life of the anchorite saint are portrayed by means of the panels of the triptych, succesive vignettes which illustrate a literary narration. In this work as in others, the narrative sense finds another appropriate vehicle in the hidden premonitory and allegorical symbols we have already discussed.

In the group of works with visionary themes about the Last Judgement and man's ultimate destiny, the narration of the discourse is made easier, and the moral nature of the paintings —emininently religious ones— finds simple means for exemplification in a repertoire of new vignettes, examples of universal validity. The narrative devices of Bosch already appear in the four round panels of his early table of the *Seven Deadly Sins* Death, Judgement, Paradise and Hell. If he resorts in the first three circles to iconographically traditional models and keeps a unity between the scenes painted, it is in Hell that, as is only logical, Bosch unfurls all his imagination. Hell is a place of suffering, but not in

the abstract, that is, it is portrayed as as place of specific punishments, each of them fitted to the different sins committed by the damned soul. This Dantesque typology of punishments and sins allows the artist to develop his infernal vision in the form of a compendium of torture scenes, naturally physical rather than moral. The didactic and illustrative nature of these is underlined by the handwritten captions which accompany each type of punishment and refer directly to the transgression of the divine laws and commandments (specifically the so-called deadly or capital sins). Given that this is the subject of the central circular panel of the table, this anti-naturalistic device could have been avoided as it is more suitable to a moralizing print than to a pictorial table. However, Bosch did not do this and keeps up this type of anachronic explanatory conventionalism.

This typology, in this case of the future dead (who will receive their deserved reward or punishment), appears again in his following visionary works, his fragmentary panels of the *Death of the Reprobate* and *Death of the Just* in New York, or the *Death of the Miser* in Washington. If in the first two of these death has already occurred and the soul of the departed is assaulted by devils or angels, in the latter the moment of passing is portrayed (as in the former Table), and is treated almost as a scene of manners. In the former the different stages of the dead man's soul's progress are portrayed in multiple sequences framed within a single scene; in the latter, the generic nature of the portrayal eliminates the ubiquity of the sinner but does not eliminate the subsidiary scenes narrated by the vital and spiritual environment of the dying miser.

These common features are repeated in later works and are more highly developed from a figurative and conceptual point of view, such as in the *Visions of the Hereafter* in Venice, the *Last Judgements* in Munich, Vienna and Bruges or in the Madrid *Garden of Delights* itself, this latter perhaps being a premonition of the Last Judgement as from the first judgement of humanity, the Universal Flood. In some of them, the left side panel portrays some of the chosen who reach Heaven; not even Bosch's enormous imaginitive capacity allows him to invent an «attractive» life in Paradise and he has to resort to an Edenic terrestrial heaven. In others, the left side panel portrays a scene of Original. Sin in which the narration of Genesis is developed through diverse episodes dotted over the landscape. In most of these triptyches, the Last Judgement, done in traditional iconography (the resurrection of the dead, as had already appeared in the Table at El Escorial, and the weighing of souls by the archangel St. Michael), is reduced to the Divine Presence which judges (with herald angels and trumpeters, sometimes the Virgin and St. John as intermediaries in the intercession and a group of saints «in communion») and then gives way to the punishmant of the damned. This scene almost entirely takes up the central panels as a prolongation of the side panel of Hell.

Some of Bosch's formal formulas are interesting on account of their originality and visual power, such as those of the Venetian triptych. They have lost the anechdotic and episodic character in good measure of other works and transform the panels in pictures of greater conceptual substance in which the painter's imagination has worked along other more abstract lines, as though they were addressed to a more cultured client than the common spectator. The number of figures in the panels begins to diminish with regard to other works and the subsidiary scenes lose much of their anechdotic character. In the *Fall of the Damned,* the fallen are dragged below towards an obscure ahd shadowy abyss accosted by demons. In *Hell* a burning landscape of lakes and rivers, a figure tormented by a devil meditates as if it wanted to remember the causes of its painful plight whilst other damned at its side are undergoing their punishment or are drawn by the dark current with the water round their necks. The *Entry into Heaven* is portrayed as a large cylinder seen in perspective (marked by its concentric bands which produces its illumination against the light) towards which the souls are drawn by the rays of divine light shining from the top of the «funnel». The figures of the chosen and the angels, the souls and the incorporeal beings, seem to dissolve as they advance on their way towards the heavenly Paradise. In these three visions, the anechdotic and episodic, the narrative have all been eliminated and they are replaced by «overall» visualizations which rouse more abstract sentiments, on the strength of more connotative than denotative feelings of situations of universal meaning. In these panels Bosch's imagination soars to great heights although they have little to do with certain other works of his which are more topical and better-known.

The Triptych of the *Flood* in Rotterdam is also connected with the Venetian paintings. If in the outer circles Bosch returns to typology (the devil in the city, the devil in the country, the man who is saved and the man who is damned), the sense of ambiental, atmospheric, more spiritual and more pictorial feeling of the antediluvian and post-diluvian worlds prevails, as premonltlons of the Last Judgement and, therefore, with the same eschatalogical meaning. It is possible that this subject, seen through apparently more optimistic eyes although with a similar final intention, could be the same as that of the *Garden of Delights.* But in this triptych, the narrative, quintessential structure eliminates all traces of sensitive visualisation. In both works, nevertheless, the didactic formula of the representation of «historical events» is kept as a premonition of universal, permanent, albeit latent, situations.

In the fourth group of works in which we have divided the painting of the master of Hertogenbosch, the subjects of which are strictly allegorical, there is a tendency to camouflage their ultimate contents with subjects which, at first sight, could appear to be profane but which invariably contain a moral and didactic purpose. The generic scenes of the table of the *Seven Deadly Sins* displays this in a very obvious way, showing the different types of sin in their most customary aspects and seeking in the proximity of the example, the easy identification of the spectator with the protagonists of each of the vignettes. Any spectator can see himself reflected in one or another picture (even the shaping of the table in radial compartments, one for each sin —with its caption— brings to mind contemporary practical manuals of confession and the central circular panel appears to attempt to substitute one of the typical circular mirrors of the time). In this way, as sin is brought near to everyday reality, the spectator is able to examine his own conscience. The scenographic and anechdotic detail and the echo of human sins in the animal world (the dog sleeping by the fire, the cur which envies its fellow's bone) or the irrational human world (the child as the glutton's apprentice) reinforce and vivify the artist's intentions, who, on the other hand, displays a remarkable capacity for capturing human reality in its daily, vulgar course. The satirical and ridiculing tone, with which Bosch covers sinful actions —a motive for mockery and scorn— in turn facilitates the effect of hypothetical rejection by the spectator. To the invitation to penitence and the purpose of improvement through attrition rather than through contrition, an invitation is added, based on social conventions or «what the neighbours will say».

The Conjurer in Saint-Germain-en Laye, which shows a scene from everyday life of the time to denounce the credulity of many, both in profane and terrestrial as in spiritual matters, abounds in this; in it there are even portrayals of those who mock at the credulous for their ingenuity (or take advantage to rob them). In the *Ship of Fools* in the Louvre, *The*

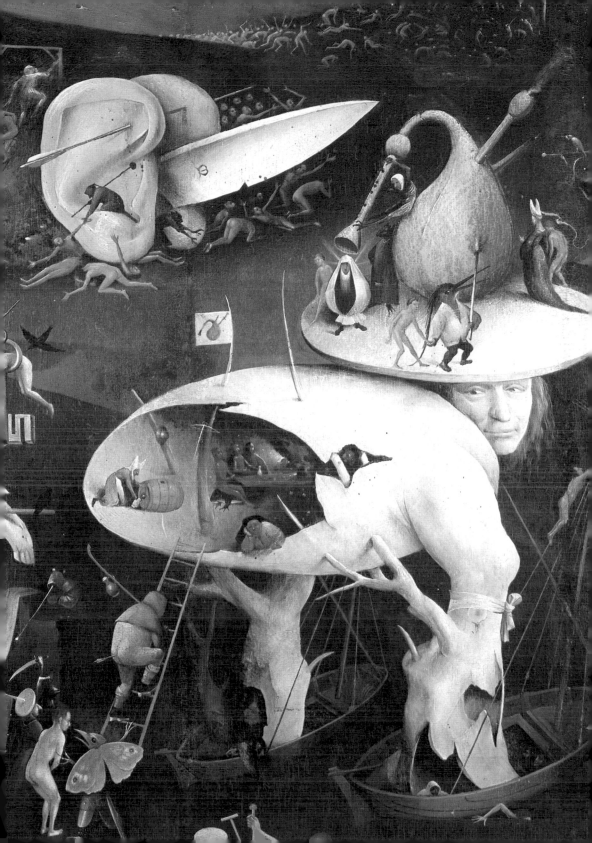

Stone of Madness in Madrid or the *Allegory of Pleasures* in The Hague, whilst the devices of the generic scene are not abandoned nor its mocking tone, there is a tendency to other methods which are more based on literary narrations or on traditional representations such as that of the Dutch battle between Carnival and Lent.

In these works Bosch approaches more pure allegory and forgets the «rhetorical» technique of visual periphrasis when he portrays a concept or an idea by means of its materialization in the environment of man's everyday life. Within this new formulism, the *Prodigal Son* in Rotterdam may also be included; this is a variation on the theme of the wanderer through life of *The Haycart* and which may well be an illustration of Freidank's saying «I know not who I am nor where I am going», referring of course to the path and end of man's life.

The theme of the unheeding madman (such as the antediluvians of Noah's time), which were so familiar at the time thanks to the 14th century mystics and contemporary humanists, with their consequent oblivion of religion and the sacred and their blind interest in the terrestrial, is developed in *The Haycart* in Madrid. If one may find its literary source in Flemish proverbs which identify the haycart with the struggle for the futile goods of this world, the details of the picture are far removed from the world of proverbs and fit neatly into the ambit of the anechdotic, the generic scene, the satirical vignette. The cart runs between Paradise and Hell like a portrayal of man's life-story; the scene is full of smaller scenes which bear witness to the madness of all states, classes or social strata, all ages, trades and conditions, in a painting of collective madness, but at the time one which is profoundly analysed and classified in its protagonists, inclinations, points of view, temptations and falls.

In short, the often boring and pedantic trappings of the moral literature of the time against the vices of the time loses its leaden monotony in the hands of our painter. Bosch's works are attractive, even amusing for the humorous satires they contain, disconcerting for the mysteries which they still harbour in many aspects and, above all, they are an inexhaustable repertory and of a variety which cannot flag of fantastic images, anechdotes and stories, symbols, literary narrations or sensitive visualizations which will always enrich us and leave us wondering about the creative prodigy of his portentous visual imagination.

THE BATTLE OF CARNIVAL AND LENT. Cramer Gallery, The Hague.

119

The first problem which arises in a study of Bosch's stylistic evolution is that of his starting-point. The lack of information as to his artistic training has allowed scholars of his painting to seek for influence both in the Flemish ambient in the strict sense and in the Dutch, between whose orbits and main artistic centres the Brabantine city of Hertogenbosch was situated. Thus, the influence of Dirk Bouts of Haarlem (10), of Geergten tot Sint Jan, also of Haarlem (11), of the master of the *Virgo inter Virgines* of Delft (a painter and graphic designer who was almost expressionist and whose word is charged with the impact of popular prints) (12), of Roger van der Weyden of Brussels (13), of the Master of Flémalle (14) or Jan van Eyck (15) himself, have been put forward. The damned of the *Last Judgement* of this latter in New York have been put forward as a specific sources of Boschian demonology. Or, widening the sphere of influences, the names of Martin Schongauer (16), or the Upper Rhenish master E. S. (17) or Erhard Reeuwich of Utrecht, identified with the master of the *Hausbuch* and the Amsterdam Cabinet (18), and the famous illustrator (of subjects which also appear in Bosch) of the «Pilgrimages in the Holy Land» (1986) of Breydenbach have all been put forward.

Today, since Baldass's research (19), and that of Benesh (20) and De Tolnay (21), critics are inclined to accept the hypothesis of local training within the family environment of the van Akens and, therefore and despite the dates, still involved in the pre-Eyckian International Gothic style, in the «soft style» *(weicher Stil)*. De Tolnay speculates with the hypothesis of a school of Hertogenbosch, which was provincial and re-

(10) L. von Baldass. *Hieronymus Bosch.* Vienna, 1943.
(11) H. Dollmayr. «Hieronymus Bosch und die Darstellung...». *Jahrbuch der Künsthistorischen Sammlungen,* 1898.
(12) W. Cohen. «Hieronymus Bosch» in *Thieme-Becker Künstlerlexicon,* IV. 1910. p. 386 ff.
(13) Carl Justi. *Miscellaneen aus drei Jahrhunderten spanischen Künstlenens.* 1908 (formerly 1899), II, p. 61-93. Formerly as an article in the *Jahrbuch der preussischen Künstsammlungen.*
(14) H. Hymams. *«Les Musées de Madrid. Le Musée du Prado IV. Gazette des Beaux-Arts,* 1893. «Ecoles du Nord. Les Primitifs. La Renaissance.»
(15) Baldass. *op. cit.*
(16) Max Dvorák. *Künstgeschichte als Geitesgeschichte,* Munich, 1924.
(17) On Master E. S. see M. Geisberg. *Die Kupferstiche des Meisters E. S.* Berlin, 1924.
(18) Dirk Bax. *Hieronymus Bosch, his picture-writing deciphered.* Rotterdam, 1979.
(19) L. von Baldass. «Betrachtungen zum Werke des Hieronymus Bosch». *Jahrbuch der Künsthistorischen Sammlungen in Wien,* 1. 1926. p. 103-22.
(20) Otto Benesch. «H. Bosch and the thinking of the late Middle Ages». *Konsthistorisk Tidskrift,* 1957. p. 21-42 and p. 103-27.
(21) Charles De Tolnay. *Hieronymus Bosch,* Basle, 1937.

tardative, and as antecedents of Hieronymus Bosch's style studied the works of the van Aken dynasty and others produced in the city of Brabant. In this way he analysed certain frescoes in the collegiate church of St. John (such as a *Tree of Jesse,* a *St. Nicholas* and a *Saint Peter and James)* of the beginning of the 15th century and, especially the *Crucifixion with Donators* of 1444, a fresco which has been attributed to Bosch's grandfather, Jan van Aken.

According to this theory, the starting point for Bosch's art must have been the fresco tradition of the High Gothic style (ca. 1390-1400) and the International Gothic (ca. 1400-1420), removed from the chronological and pictorial approach of the Flemish innovations which occurred round about the second third of the 15th century. This is the training which the works of Bosch's early period display and which may be dated between 1475 and 1480/5 (22). These first works still show reminiscences of the brilliant colourism of International Gothic and also of the school of Haarlem. At the same time, they also display a timid assimilation of the advances in the field of landscape and perspective of the primitive Flemish painters. This is Bosch's period of greatest simplification, from the folds in the drapery of his figures to his simple, geometric, rhomboid compositional lay-outs. There appear, however, some of his most personal characteristics: his didactic sense, his lack of interest in monofocal perspective and his tendency to «knightly visions», his exaggeration of reality (according to Gothic popular and traditional conventions), his taste for «ridicule», his mises-en-scène of the sinful in everyday, generic guise or his attainment of monumental effects by means of blocking the backgrounds of his scenes with a «wall». Charactieristics which fall outside this period are his uncertain drawing, his interest in architectonic interiors, the independence of figures and landscape (overlapping with difficulty), the poverty and stiffness of his figures' movements, his «pure» colouring without toning, or his later angular treatment of drapery.

Works of a profane nature belong to this first period, such as *The Stone of Madness* in the Prado or *The Sorcerer* or *The Magician* in Saint-Germain-en-Laye (with its composition based on the contrast between a *mass* and a *«miraculous» figure* of the Italian 12th century tradition), or works of a more strictly religious nature such as the table of the *Seven*

---

(22) De Tolnay's chronology in *op. cit.* and re-editions; J. Combe. *Jérôme Bosch,* Paris, 1964, suggests the most restricted chronology in the length of the periods.

Deadly Sins in the Prado, *The Marriage of Canaan* in Rotterdam, the *Epiphany* in Philadelphia, the *Crucifixion* in Brussels (a late work according to certain critics) or the *Ecce Homo's* in Frankfurt and Boston. In the *Table* in Madrid, Bosch links it with 15th century engravings, as far as its structure is concerned. The iconographies of the round corner panels have also been related to xylographs of the time, *Death* in particular with a picture by master E. S. for the «Ars Moriendi», or *Hell* with Flemish engravings (such as those from the «Calendrier du Berger») in the Italian 12th century tradition. The *Marriage of Canaan* displays the ambiental influence of the *Last Supper* in Louvain by Dirk Bouts (compositions with an L-shaped table had already appeared in the Italian 14th century and the Flemish 15th) and by the Master of Flémalle, in the small figures and implied space (23), The *Crucifixion* brings to mind the work of his grandfather Jan (24); the *Epiphany* recalls the compositions of Robert Campin and his disciple Jacques Daret. The *Ecce Homo's* (the one in Boston perhaps a workshop painting) is likewise connected with contemporary engravings, above all in its figure of Christ.

For other critics, the Philadelphia *Epiphany* or the Brussels *Crucifixion* belonged to an intermediate period, between 1480 and 1485 in which a greater sense of movement appears, Bosch combines curved forms from his first period with other angular spikey ones, among which the broken folds of his figures' draperies stand out and which were so typical of primitive Flemish painting. In this stage of transition to his mature stylistic period, there are still echoes of his first form in the stiffness and schematization in the distribution of compositional elements. His technique is less refined than it was to be later in a far more elaborate form. An increasing capacity for impact is to be observed, the drawing becomes gradually more and more fluid and expressive, albeit at the same time there are remains of his juvenile vacillating and bold style, above all in the landscape in which he avoids the type of lay-out hitherto popularized. In his boldness he approaches the works of the beginning of the century, those which came from the provincial artistic currents.

---

(23) The name «space by implication» or «interior by implication» has been given to the method of representing an interior space based above all on the effect of depth created by a violently receding floor, at the cost of the disappearance of most of the side walls of the interior, whether there is an architectonic or merely neutral background or not.
(24) With additions, for example, from the art of Roger van der Weyden (the feet of Christ and the airy drapery of purity floating in decorative manner, opposed to the stillness of the crucified figure, in such a way as to underline the dramatic effect of the composition).

TABLE OF THE SEVEN DEADLY SINS. *Wrath*. Prado Museum, Madrid.

His mature period for De Tolnay covers the works of the years between 1480 and 1510 and, for Combre, for example, those of between 1485 and 1505 (25). The works of this central period represent the elaboration and development of the traits which had appeared so far. The most famous works of this period are *The Ship of Fools* in the Louvre, the *Haycart* and *The Garden of Delights* in the Prado, the *Triptych of the Flood* in Rotterdam, the altar-piece of the *Temptations of Saint Anthony* in Lisbon, the *Last Judgement* in Vienna or the Venetian *Visions of the Hereafter*. His painting is by now *alla prima,* full of expressivity, with a flowing and immediately recognisable style. The central subject of his panels is fragmented into a myriad allusive sub-themes in which the representations and symbols mingle inextricably: the «bugs» begin to appear (till then more or less mostrous animals but isolated instances and with no mixture of human elements). Each figure possesses a meaning which the form tends to underline. In each image, the allusive expression of a symbol, a semioccult concept may be discovered.

In some of these works by the master of Hertogenbosch, there is still a dependence on previous engravings to a certain extent, although they gradually grow independent of the original source. Master E. S. and his engravings for the «Ars moriendi» underly *The Death of the Miser* in Washington, but Bosch incorporates a «proscenium» in the foreground of his composition in the manner of the master of Flémalle and Roger van der Weyden, using alien sources which are no mere quotation. In *The Ships of Fools* in Paris, there is influence from the «Stultiferae naviculae...» (1498) by Jodocus Badius but what in this latter was purely linear, has been transformed into light and colour in Bosch. In *Christ Carrying the Cross* in Vienna there is the influence of one of Allaert de Hameel's engravings (in turn influenced by Jan van Eyck and, in the ultimate analysis by Giotto through the Franco-Flemish tradition) in the composition and in the crown of heads in works by Meister Franke and the German tradition of the middle of the century. The *Ecce Homo* in a Swiss private collection echoes one of the xylographs in the *Grand Passion* by Albert Dürer, converting this latter's plastic sense into a pictorial one.

On the other hand, the stylistic or compositional influences of his great triptyches are much more difficult to place. His small figures may be derived from miniatures (Hours of Turin-Milan, Hours of Chantilly), as

---

(25) One of the most recent studies on Bosch, by Patrick Reuterswärd. *Hieronymus Bosch.* Uppsala, 1970, suggests another new chronology: before 1490, 1490-1504 and 1504-1516.

likewise some of his isolated subjects (such as some of those in the *Garden of Delights)* may be related to the illustrations of texts such as those by Reeuwich or those of the «Livre des Merveilles de Monde» in the Morgan Library. The mental visions of the Lisbon *St. Anthony* likewise recall miniatures such as the Book of Hours by John of Bedford in the London British Museum. However, it is here that Bosch's originality shines out to best effect. In the Portuguese triptych, his brushstrokes tend once more to be stratified, albeit without losing the fluidity and suppleness he was to display in the *Haycart,* whilst the drapery waves in curved forms which recall the decorative architecture of *flamboyant* Gothic. The images are even focussed with greater intensity. The composition tends to a continuous development, space becomes a phantasmagorical element and his paintings remind one of stellar constellations of brilliant episodes, accurate in the extreme thanks to a brush which captures the subtlest fading of an outline or movement. Detail is presented with tremendous severity with an imagination that nevertheless preserves all the unseizable fluidity of Bosch's line and his abundant complexity. In the Philippine *Garden,* this type of technique of Bosch's reaches its peak, a technique which is perhaps at one and the same time the most medieval and most modern to our eyes, as in the *Last Judgement* in Vienna. The mysterious scenes, commonplaces of mystic and humanistic literature, rather than exponents of heterodoxy or simple satirical brushstrokes, are full of the motifs which were to make Bosch universally famous and one of the imaginative sources of western culture, with his devils mixed with human, animal and vegetable elements or his mineralized landscapes in his vegetable world.

In the *Triptych of the Flood* Hieronymus Bosch breaks with traditional images, totally inventing his own —on the basis of biblical texts— not only in details, and opens up his own very personal path to landscape, which in these panels is almost an idependent pictorial genre and which in the grisaille of the *Garden of Delights* —with its recently created or recently flooded globe and its lustre or its rainbow— becomes the first pure landscape of modern painting. In the Venetian *Visions,* another of his most original and independent works, and one of the most innovating from another point of view, Bosch substitutes the «objective», traditional images of heavenly and infernal hierarchies «by subjective visions which correspond to the (literary) conceptions of the great mystics and which only exist in the inner world» (26).

---

(26) Ch. De Tolnay. *Hieronymus Bosch.* London, 1966. p. 30.

THE CONCERT OF THE EGG *(frag.)*. Palais des Beaux-Arts, Lille.

Another type of works give way to his last period. These are difficult to assign to one or another stage, such as some of his scenes from the Passion of Christ or images of saints. Thus, the *Christ Carrying the Cross* in the Madrid Royal Palace, the *Crownings with Thorns* in London and El Escorial (these latter with his half-figures and fine modelling of the faces despite the «bestialization» of some of his faces), the *Saint John the Evangelist at Patmos* in Berlin, the *St. Jerome Penitent* in Ghent, the *St. John the Baptist* in the Madrid Lázaro-Galdiano Museum, the *St. Christopher* in Rotterdam and the Venetian altar-pieces of *St. Julia* or *St. Liberata* and the *Hermits* (St. Jerome, St. Anthony and St. Giles), these two latter works with a curious granulated technique. In these paintings, which display the most typical subject matter and iconography of the time, traditional elements, borrowings (for example, a similar composition to that of certain engravings by Master E. S. or Schongauer in the Berlin *St. John)* and Bosch's own creation (the composition of *St. Jerome* lying on the ground in prayer, in Ghent), all live side-by-side.

In the late works of our painter, those after 1510, the search for the Brabantine master ends with the immediate and intensely colouristic evidence of his forms. A certain spiritual distension becomes manifest, it seems as if he frees himself little by little from his former religious nightmares, that serenity provided by a firmly followed ideal programme is displayed, thus intensifying his lucid and intense formal visualisation. Bosch lightens his palette and his figures come nearer in majesty to those of Eyck's works or those of the Master of Flémalle, albeit without altogether appeasing his former uneasiness, which detracts unity from a disconcerting calm. Thus in the *Adoration of the Magi* in the Prado Museum or in many of his paintings of penitent saints.

In this latter work, as in a ricochet effect after his hypothetical trip to Italy which we have already discussed in full, Bosch turns his eyes to Jan van Eyck and Robert Campin, the creators of primitive Flemish painting. The posture of the Virgin and Child recall the *Virgin of Chancellor Rollin,* by Jan, as do the movements and treatment of drapery. The composition, with its bird's-eye-view landscape, recalls the Dijon *Nativity* by the Master of Flémalle or the altar of *St. Columba* in Munich by Roger van der Weyden, his disciple and near rival. The monsters have almost completely disappeared in this phase of his art; the figures take on a volume and mass hitherto unusual and which approach the most innovating currents of Flemish 15th century painting, being heirs to the sculpture of

Claus Sluter. However, there still remain certain previous traits which are typically his: the spacial discontinuity between the three panels or the details (such as St. Joseph warming the Child's nappies) which may go back to pre-Eyckian art. The triptych of the *Epiphany* of Anderlecht prolongs this type of Bosch's work.

The influence of the great artists of the recently closed century (Geertgen, Bouts, above all) is also felt in the *Temptations of St. Anthony* in New York, with its numeric diminishing and its expressive intensity of the tempting monsters, the subordination of the colours to a general, harmonic colouring of only two tones. The *St. Anthony* in the Prado Museum links up with this latter work and, above all as far as colouring is concerned, the *Prodigal Son* in Rotterdam, with its tendency to monochrome and its fine fading technique. Both works contribute new solutions, on the other hand, to more traditional iconographs on these subjects.

Nevertheless, compared to this moment at which Jeroen van Aken achieves a balance between his creative power and the weight of contemporary artistic tradition (as may also be seen in his canvases of St. John of Hertogenbosch), there comes another at which other later works seem quite opposed to this inner equilibrium and calm or, at least, which reverse its meaning. The *Carrying the Cross* in Ghent or the *Christ before Pilate* in Princeton display a mixture of uneasy, active evil and an ambiguous, dual, perhaps inexplicable calm, within the framework of a new type of composition to which we have already referred in detail. The horrifying caricatures, the profiles, the half-figures or heads and busts, the *horror vacui,* the lack of space, with their oppressive sense, are opposed to the calm of Christ, Pilate or Veronica —of a very different kind—. Movement or gesture, disinterest or self-absorption are shown in the same panels as if frozen, detained for an instant in a precarious situation, as though this were a calm which must soon give way to a tempest, darkening the painter's palette, and overhung by clouds which threaten a torrent of rains and evils.

Bosch's activity comes to a close with these works. After this attempt at a stylistic analysis in evolution, is it possible to speak of evolution in the case of Bosch's work? Not in a traditional sense, of course. On the other hand, it is hard to agree. There is no linear, continuous or «logical» development. The most medieval elements of his painting do not correspond to his early years. The influences of other artists and other works seem to occur without any obvious reason; they crop up then vanish for a time and return later for no plausible reason. Throughout Bosch's three great periods, there is no stylistic unity either. Different sub-periods could be pointed to —impossible to specify from a chronological point of view— which seem totally opposed to each other. It is sometines difficult to set limits to one of his most typical traits; at others it is hard to accept the dates supplied by scholars of his work; at others, the jumps in time seem explicable. His plurality is always excessive.

Yet, however different and opposed to one another Bosch's works may be, they all bear his peculiar hallmark and stylistic common denominators may be traced in their ensemble. All of them respond mysteriously to one hand and one brain, those of the mysterious, unique, unitary, plural and contradictory Hieronymus Bosch.

IV

THE CONTENT
OF BOSCH'S WORKS

Jeroen van Aken is above all a man of his time who shows himself to be in his works a biting critic of the society in which he lived as a painter. We have attempted to explain the iconography of his works and his biography by making him the protagonist of each of the subjects expounded in his paintings: for some he is a heretic of the *Brotherhood of the Free Spirit;* to the contrary, others believe him to be an orthodox Catholic; whilst others think he belonged to a masonic sect, there are those who see in him one possessed by the devil; there is no lack of those who take him to be an alchemist, erotically obsessed or a moralist. As may be appreciated, judgement on the artist is contradictory and yet in all of them there is some element of reason, inasfar as the judgement passed is based upon a consideration of the artist as judge and participant. Who could today assert that a painter or photographer is the protagonist of the iconographs of his works? On the whole, he is merely a witness or a critic of his surroundings and the 15th century painter is still far removed from the commited artist of our 20th century. We must judge the painter of Hertogenboch in exactly the same way.

As we shall see below, we can appreciate in his work the typical vitalism of a society in crisis, in the bosom of which —customs, myths, symbols and medieval witchcraft— the seed of Renaissance humanism was to be gestated. Heresy, faith; morals, alchemy, witchcraft, eroticism, the demoniac, and, as a binding force for all, religion, were all constitutional elements of this time and society. It is for this reason that Bosch's pictorial work seems impregnated by all these subjects, because they bore witness to them.

It should not be thought that judgement of Jeroen van Aken is an exception: similarly contradictory critiques are passed on Fernando de Rojas or M. François Rabelais. Their orks, «La tragicomedia de Calixto y

Melibea» and «Gargatua and Pantagruel», the reflections of a society and epoch identical in the former and only a few decades away in the latter, display characters moved by similar themes to Bosch's. Contradictorily judged authors, accused of being active protagonists of anything that happens in their works like Rojas, Rabelais and Bosch, they are no more than artists who witness with their satire, mordacity and extraordinary fantasy a humankind distressed by the birth of a new vital conception. How close are the rebelaisian fantasies to those of Bosch's work!

We shall give herebelow a brief analysis of Bosch's iconography and in order to understand it better, we have divided it into four parts: the man of his time, «Vita Christi», the saints and glossary of symbols. In the first part, as in Pandora's box, we have gathered together a series of paintings which have as protagonist Man coetaneous with Jeroen van Aken. Here one can observe a didactic-moralizing iconology, one always subjected to Divine Will and it is not therefore unusual to see the figure of Christ or even God Himself appear as a witness or co-author of human manifestations. Jesus Christ is to be the protagonist of the paintings in the second part; there is no doubt that the iconology of these latter is directly related to the society which contemplates them and which partly influences the interpretation of the painter's mentality. In this sense, the paintings could be included in the first part, although on account of their entity we prefer to put them together in a different group. We might say the same of the third group, the saints. As we state in the introduction to this chapter, some saints are so close to men in their iconographic conception that we could find their figures among the people of the Brabantine society in which Bosch lived.

In the iconographic interpretation in the first place and its iconological analysis in the second, we have preferred to explain the general idea of the picture before going on to a detailed analysis of all the iconographed elements. In the first place, and in order to facilitate interpretation, we have tried to keep along the lines of historical rigour. In the second place, on account of the space devoted on these pages to the subject, it would be impossible to summarize the extremely rare and versatile iconographs represented in the paintings. The general intention of most of Bosch's work is comprehensible: there are literary and plastic testimonies which allow us access to his message in general terms. The doubt or the problem arises when one wishes to interpret the slightest details by wanting to subordinate them to a certain interpretation, for they have

lost their value as symbols in many instances —they are no more than mere decorative elements— or their emblematic versatily is so varied that each of the versions given to them, however disparate they may be, might have been taken into account by Bosch. It would be a good thing for the reader to complete his study of the paintings with an analysis of the most representative symbols reproduced in the glossary at the end.

THE MAN OF HIS TIME

The social critic, the moralizing spirit —here we have the basic idea behind the chief paintings of the master of Hertogenbosch, not the *Adamite* heretic that Wilhelm Fraenger (1) thought he saw. It seems enlightening that a spirit so zealous of the Christian Roman Catholic faith as Philip II should be the greatest collector of his works. In 16th century Spain, troubled as it was by problems of Christian orthodoxy, it would be unconceivable that the champion of Christianity should keep for his recreation the work of a heretic or sexual maniac. One of his first commentators, Fray José de Sigüenza, did nor hesitate to point out the ethical nature— that is moralizing nature, of his work when he wrote:... «behold in them —his works— almost all the Sacraments and states and degrees of the Church, from the Pope to the lowest, *two points over which all heretics stumble,* and he painted them in many ways and with great esteem, for if he were a heretic he would not have done so... I want to show now... that his paintings are not follies... and to say once and for all that they are painted satires of the sins and misdeeds of men» (2).

We shall see later on, when we analyse his pictorial production work by work, that there is nothing in them which could be suspected of heresy but a great deal of the religious reality (Christian-Catholic) of the time. If on account of interpretation problems we are in doubt as to a certain specific symbol, the ensemble of the subject confirms its orthodoxy for evil —sin in its widest sense— always receives the corresponding punishment. Evil is always portrayed through deformity, the monstrous, following the medieval tradition. In this same sense the shaping of the spaces is shown: ordered, correct, in harmonious colours in the creation of

---

(1) On Bosch and the Adamites, see: «Die Hochzeit zu Kana. Ein Dokument semitischer Gnosis bei Hjeronimus Bosch», Berlin, 1950 and «Bosch», Dresden, 1975.
(2) See note 10, Chapter 1.

the divine hand; disorder and confusion in Satanic possessions. In this sense it is enlightening to compare the paradises and hells of the most important triptyches.

Through his paintings, Bosch attempts to correct the institutions, habits, although this is not his own originality but merely that he moulds in images what a select minority was bringing about in European society of the 15th and 16th centuries. As Huizinga has written, the whole of life was so drenched in religion that the distance between the sacred and profane threatened to vanish at any moment. The elevated spirituality of the Middle Ages was by then in decadence, religious sentiment had become denaturalized, if not weakened, by a progressive profanation. The *devotio moderna,* theologians and clergyman such as the exegete Frenchman Lefèvre d'Etaples (1450-1538) (3), the clergy of Windesheim in the Netherlands, the mystic Johann von Staupitz (1460-1524) in Germany, reacted against this current. All of them tried to purge the Church of useless ceremonies and sacrileges, and to encourage the survival of popular faith. To this end they thought it was necessary to return to the sources, the general Biblical principles and to the evangelical ones in particular. In short, they made for the *pure Christianity* divulged during Bosch's lifetime by Erasmus of Rotterdam (1487-1538). Jeroen van Aken moralizes, criticises with satire and irony the men of his social environment. In order to portray his iconography he does not hasitate to resort to the popular, he does not even reject the obscene and sordid in order to be truer to life, but the basis of punishment, the moralizing spirit, is inspired by evangelical principles or ecclesiastic dictates pertaining to the reformist élite of the end of the 15th century and the painter does not hesitate to transcribe specific Biblical quotations which explain the moral paradigm of some of his works (*Table of the Seven Deadly Sins*). In certain instances, the Biblical principle seems non-existent, albeit an exegetical analysis of the popular proverb which inspires the composition and immediately shows its relationship with the Bible. To this effect the comment we make below on the *Triptych of the Hay* should be read. These resources from the popular to clarify principles of a moral kind were very much to the taste of the preachers of the time.

The cosmic vision shown in Bosch's work comes between the two topical and typical conceptions which Burckhardt attributes to the medie-

---

(3) In 1494, his work «Ars moralis» appeared.

val and Renaissance worlds, that is, between the theocentrism of the Middle Ages and the anthropocentrism of the Renaissance. If we look at the *Seven Deadly Sins,* we see how, both from a plastic and ideological point of view, humanity revolves around divinity. *The Man* of the Boymans-van Beunigen Museum seems to be pictorial evidence of Renaissance humanism. He is not the undifferentiated man of the jumbled, entangled and confused humanity of the *Garden of Delights* but he is the individual and his own experience of life. The obvious explanation of this co-existence of counterposed human conceptions is justified by the biological reality of the painter who lived through years of change and could not extricate himself from the conceptual ambivalence which characterized all human manifestations of the time. In an already mentioned contemporary work of literature, «La tragicomedia de Calisto y Melibea» (1498), we see how the same vital duality we have just mentioned is displayed in it. The experiential interpretation of the lovers, Calisto and Melibea, is purely Renaissance, whilst the world of Celestina and her servants is in tha purest medieval tradition.

A conflictive point in Bosch iconography, and one which certain critics use to accuse him of heresy, is his anti-clericalism (4). When one sees friars as the protagonists of lasciviousness in the *Ship of Fools,* the *Garden of Delights,* etc., or of any of the flaws of society as portrayed by Jeroen van Aken, this is no more than a plastic manifestation of something quite normal in mysticism, particularly within the Flemish church itself and in European mysticism in general. Erasmus wrote in his «Praise of Madness», *monachus non es pietas.* The fragment from Rabelais which I reproduce here seems highly suggestive to me: «And how is Abbot Tranchelion the great drinker? And the other monks, are they leading the good life? God's Body! They kiss your wives whilst you are off on pilgrimages... That's how you get the pox if on your return you don't find them all pregnant, for the shade of an abbey belfry is highly fertile» (5). The literary passage coincides in irony and intentionality with the caricatures of monks by Bosch in the *Triptych of the Hay,* the *Triptych of the Temptations of St. Anthony* in the Museum Nacional de Arte Antiga in Lisbon, etc.

---

(4) For some authors there is both clerical and anti-clerical subject-matter in Bosch. For the study of same, see Lucien Fèbvre, «Le prolème de l'incroyance au XVIe siècle. La religion de Rabelais», Paris, 1968, p. 17 and 18. For Fraenger, this antithesis is justified because Bosch worked for two different patrons: the Church and *a revolutionary adversary* (W. Fraenger, «The Millenium of Hieronymus Bosch. Outlines of a new interpretation». London, 1952, p. 18.

(5) F. Rabelais, «Gargantua and Pantagruel», vol. I, P. 121-122 (ed. Barcelona, 1971).

Let us not quote only characters that might be judged to be of doubtful orthodoxy. The same criticism of certain sectors of the clergy may be seen in the writings of Johan Gerson, Dionisio Cartujano, Nicholas de Clémanges, Pierre d'Ailly, etc. A century later, in over-clerical Spain, Friar José de Sigüenza, upon contemplating the satirical treatment given to the clergy in the *Triptych of the Hay,* found nothing heretical at all in it. Once more the master of Hertogenbosch does no more than transfer to his paintings quite normal ideas for the men of his time.

Eroticism, perhaps erotic pranks, may form part of the most suggestive side of his output, but here neither does he move away from what the ecclesiastical moralizers wrote or preached. From the beginnings of the *Gothic age,* theologians and preachers had been introducing in their works tales, metaphors and similes which had become gradually more and more fiery and in which the carnal and the spiritual became confused. One might say that they chose this language to draw the attention of their listeners better. Licence in customs among these latter was absolute, illegitimate births were a habitual practice of the time: Duke Philip had eighteen bastard children, the Bishop of Liège Johan van Heinsberg fourteen or fifteen and as many as sixty-three are given for John II of Cleves. The strange thing is that these carnal sinners were at the same time profoundly religious. Philip the Good an insatiable lecher, fasted on bread and water four days a week and his religious devotion was extreme. The art of religious finality also echoes this wave of eroticism and we may observe how, at the same time as religious literature draws comparisons between the Virgin Mary and Eve, in sculpture and painting the Virgin takes on sensual forms which bring her nearer to Venusian ideals. A highly significant example is the Virgin of the famous *Diptych of Melun* in which Fouquet (1420-1481) portrayed the famous breasts of Agnes Sorel, the mistress of Charles VII. Alain de la Roche (1428-1475), a famous preacher, in order to draw the attention of his audience better and to be more persuasive, introduced obscenely sensual images into the sermons. If from the pulpit there came erotic images, what would Jeroen van Aken not do in his paintings? Moved by a spirit of pictorial verism, he portrays scenes of a people who, as we have seen, was especially inclined to sensuality. However, carnal sin is never left in Bosch's work without its corresponding punishment, once more displaying that moralizing sense which Bosch perhaps did not feel as an artist but which had to please the client who had commissioned the work.

THE GARDEN OF DELIGHTS *(frag.).* Prado Museum, Madrid.

We spoke at the beginning of Bosch as a witness of the society in which he lived and as such we may observe through his images elements which belong to alchemy. This latter was an important factor of the spiritual ethos of the Middle Ages. Alchemy and witchcraft were confused and repeatedly persecuted by the Church, a fact which confirms their importance (6). Bosch was probably familiar with the subject and we should not forget that the visions of Tundalus had been printed in Hertogenbosch in 1484 (7). However, that he had any knowledge of aspects related to alchemy should not allow us to consider him as a practitioner of same, even more so if we bear in mind that not one of his works preserved today develops any iconograph which could lead to a complete interpretation of the alchemy type. As we shall see in the section on the «Vita Christi», the *Marriage of Canaan* (8) shows no elements whatever which break with traditional orthodox iconography of the time. Many symbols portrayed in his work are possibly related to alchemy but what is today impossible to accept is the long list of subjects adduced as proof in the most arbitrary way. We shall give here some of the motifs which are considered to be symbols from alchemy: the hollow tree, hybrids, the egg, the Virgin and the solar disc (*St. John in Patmos*), the child-Mercury (*Temptations of St. Anthony* in Lisbon), the crow, the lamb, the stone (*St. John the Baptist* in the Lázaro Galdiano Museum), the blacksmiths of the underworld, cosmic landscapes, the star of Solomon, different metals, minerals, the globe, etc. Doubtless all these subjects could have a purely alchemical symbology, but of how many other fields too? We could even accept the alchemical exegesis of the different elements but we should not forget that many of these motifs had been taken over by the vocabulary of mysticism and were then germane to this latter as in the writings of Ruysbroeck (1294-1381).

Together with these interpretations, which are more or less congruent, with the contribution of certain texts and images which allow us to corroborate them in space and time, there exist visions of Jeroen van

(6) This is the epoch in which Pope Innocent VIII issued the notorious bull «Sumnis desiderantes affectibus» (1484), to combat the spread of magical practices. Shortly after, the terrible «Malleus Maleficarum» was published in Strasburg (1487), in which witches are cruelly attacked.

(7) A Dutch edition had already appeared, «Het boek van Tondalus vysioen» in 1482. This work was of Irish origin: the knight Tundalus had lived in the 12th century and his spirit travelled in the hereafter for three days. This is an obscure vision which is one of the sources of visionary and demoniac iconography.

(8) The sideboard portrayed in this picture has been taken as the altar of an initiate sect. See Eugène Causeliet «L'Alchimie et le Mutus Liber».

Aken and the iconography of his work which are purely subjective and under the sway of fashion and the forms of later critics. These judgements lose all value when the circumstances in vogue which have given rise to them have been surpassed; as may well be understood, they are purely arbitrary for it is never valid for a historian to judge the past by the parametres of a different epoch. Critics did not hesitate to apply *Freudian psycho-analysis* when this latter came into fashion (9). The development of drugs as from the fifties in our society has led Robert L. Delevoy to attempt an explanation of the Bosch phenomenon as due to the effects of the so-called «witches unction», the formula of which is contained in a 16th century work. This position consists of a hallucinatory drug (10).

Throughout this brief introduction, I have tried to show that the intentionality of Bosch's iconography, in such compromising subjects as the so-called heretical aspects, the anticlerical, erotic and alchemical ones, is no more than the transfer into images of the reformist content of Flemish *devotio moderna* and of a series of religious personages who concurred in the so-called *pure Christianity* of Erasmus of Rotterdam. And we should have no doubt that in the 15th century these ideas were still within Roman Catholic orthodoxy.

Without a doubt there is a marked difference between the transcendence of the Latin writing of the reformist clergy and that of the paintings of the master of Hertogenbosch. Only an intellectual minority can have access to the former, but Bosch's images, impregnated as they are by popular experience, are open to all people who contemplate them. To this effect, Bosch does no more than fulfill in his works the didactic and moralizing tradition imposed on ecclesiastical painting by St. Gregory: images in temples should serve as instruction to the uneducated. I shall therefore end by stating that Jeroen van Aken divulged in his images a moralizing and reformist spirit which could only thus be assimilated by the common people (11).

---

(9) See De Tolnay's work.

(10) Robert L. Delevoy, «Bosch», Geneva 1960, p. 76.

(11) Only by examining the miniatures in the books of the 15th and 16th centuries can we find the precedents of most of Bosch's fantastic iconographs. These books, which pertained to select minorities were not within reach of the common people and perhaps Bosch found in them the images which were to serve him for the divulging of the intellectual principles of these minorities.

THE CURE FOR MADNESS, Prado Museum, Madrid.

> ...«Things are going wrong when the wise man goes to
> operate on his own madness in a madhouse»
>
> (Flemish proverb)

This is the first known work by Bosch and one may observe in it the generic scene which characterizes a great deal of Flemish painting.

Its iconological interpretation has been extremely varied: Fraenger sees in this work the symbolic expression of castration; Brand Philip's version is even more sophisticated, of an astrological nature, the picture belonging to a series on the genealogy of the planets.

The caption in Gothic lettering reads: «Master, take out the stone; my name is castrated badger» (other authors translate the name as «simpleton»). Apart from a *posteriori* iconological digressions, the most obvious thing seems that the picture is an illustration of the Flemish proverb quoted at the beginning as Marcel Brien pointed out many years ago. In this picture, the madness and idiocy which rule the world are criticised. A quack-doctor —the funnel which is a symbol of science caricatures him— extracts a water tulip from the patient's head, in the presence of a sermoning monk and a nun astonished by the power of science

Here Bosch criticises with ferocious irony the stupidity of the people, mocked as they are by quack-doctors. The world is such a silly, mad place that people go to cure themselves to mad tricksters! Erasmus said that medicine is the art which is most closely related to madness. Some verses by Rabelais give us the literary vision of a type of similar caricature to that of Bosch's plastic one as far as formal intention is concerned, although their media are different:

> In his fly a ball,
> A racket in his hand,
> A law in his hood,
> And a jig in his heel:
> Thus are doctors all (12).

---

(12) F. Rabelais, op. cit. vol. I, p. 175.

THE SEVEN DEADLY SINS: The Redemption of Human Sin, Prado Museum, Madrid.

> «For they are a nation void of counsel, neither is there
> any understanding in them.
> O that they were wise, that they understood this, that they would con-
> sider their latter end!
> ...I will hide my face from them, I will see what
> their end shall be.»

«Deuteronomy», 32: 28, 29, 20 (13).

This is a work in which the medieval influence is notable, not only for the presence of iconographs such as the *last judgement,* but also in the moralizing intention of the ensemble and remarkably so in the explanatory captions. Bosch's fantasy is still not mature although we find the embryo of his later phantasmagories and on the whole the images correspond to generic scenes from the repertory of Flemish painting.

Bold hypotheses on the iconology of the picture have been put forward, Indian *mandalas* having even been mentioned. It seems obvious from the captions from *Deuteronomy* quoted on the work that mankind has lost his wits and that man lets himself be dragged down by sin. The deadly sins are portrayed in a central ring, in amusing generic scenes in which popular life is portrayed with charm and malice. Not all is lost, however, for in the centre, in the iris of an enormous eye which sees all, is the eye of God —*Deus videt*— and Christ appears in a cruciform nimbus —a saving image— emerging from the sepulchre and showing his stigmata. It seems obvious that the painter here refers to the redemption of sin through His passion, death —symbolized by the cruciform nimbus and stigmata— and resurrection. Christ is emerging from the grave.

Faithful Christians who were contemporaries of Bosch were not only moved by a display of the signs of Christ's passion, but they also had to be made to tremble by reminding them of man's end or the *novissimi*: death, judgement, hell and glory. These latter are painted in the four corner circles. Bosch, like the preachers of his time, wanted to make those who contemplated his works think upon death. Books such as the «Art

---

(13) Quotations reproduced by Bosch on the captions of the picture.

Invidia

de mourir», «Ars moriendi», «De quattuor Novissimis», etc. (14) were divulged with the same intention around that time. The recordatory nature of self-examination in dying well seems to have been confirmed by Kurt Pfister, when he points out that it consoled Philip II in the hour of his death (15).

THE SORCERER OR CONJURER, Municipal Museum, Saint-Germain-en-Laye.

«Whoever listens to conjurers
Will lose his money and children
Will mock him».

Together with some of the scenes of *The Seven Deadly Sins,* this work is an authentic generic subject, in which Jeroen van Aken shows himself to be a true follower of the school of Haarlem.

The painting is used to effect a biting criticism of human stupidity and credulity. It appears to illustrate the proverb we quote at the beginning. A multitude of hypotheses have been formulated as to its iconological interpretation. For Fraenger it means the ritual castration of heretics in satirical form. Brand-Philip, including the picture within a series, thinks it is the symbol of the element water, the phlegmatic temperament and the planet Moon. In my opinion the iconographic elements are too far-fetched. Why should it not be no more than the illustration of a proverb? Would this be abnormal in Flemish painting? No, not at all. I believe, as does L. Ninane (16) that all those elements considered to be symbolic, the top hat, funnels, empty balls, the owl peeping out of the basket, are tools commonly used by conjurers and which appear in the picture not out of symbolic necessity, but in order to give the necessary atmosphere for an understanding of the subject. Without a doubt it is a generic scene which the acute, incisive and malicious eye of the painter turns into a plastic epigram against human stupidity.

---

(14) For this work and the *Death of the Miser,* Bosch possibly drew inspiration from the «Ars moriendi». In 1492 A. Verard published «L'art de bien Mourir». The number of editions of «De Quattuor Novissimis» by the Cartusian monk Dionysius Rijckel, bear witness to the success of the work: more than forty Latin editions and countless French, Spanish, Flemish and Italian ones.

(15) Kurt Pfister, «Hieronimus Bosch», Kiepenheuer, Postdam, 1922.

(16) L. Ninane, «Le Siècle de Bruegel», 1963.

TABLE OF THE SEVEN DEADLY SINS. *Avarice.* Prado Museum, Madrid.

THE DEATH OF THE MISER, National Gallery of Art, Washington.

«¿Qué vale su christiandad	(What is their Christianity worth
Ni a la cruz dezir «adoro»	not even saying to the cross «I adore»,
Si con toda voluntad	If with all their might and main
adoran más de verdad	They adore in truer strain
las mujeres o el thesoro?	Women and treasure.)

«Coplas de Vita Christi»
Friar Iñigo de Mendoza.

Death is dealt with in several instances in Bosch's work: *The Death of the Reprobate, The Death of the Just Man* and, above all, in *The Seven Deadly Sins.* In this work the subject of the *novissimi* (death, judgement, hell and glory) is united to that of death. As we have already stated, the *Ars moriendi* was created in the 15th century and was intimately related to the first of the stages of the end. One might even say that it became its narrative enlargement. The people of the century, tormented as they were by the subject, nead to have it explained to them. In the *Ars moriendi,* the five temptations are mentioned with which the devil waylays the dying: doubt in faith, despair for one's sins, fondness for worldly goods, despair for one's own suffering and, finally, pride in one's own virtue. Each time that Satan shows himself in one of his temptations, there appears an angel to comfort and help the dying person in his choice.

In this iconographied picture, we see the third of these temptations. The dying man; a noble knight to judge from his arms —bottom-right— is vacillating between the cross and the bag of money offered to him by one of Satan's demons. Satan witnesses the scene from the bedstead. An angel flies to help him in his choice, there is little time left for death half-opens the door of the chamber. Bosch juxtaposes in the same space a scene from the past, a plastic device of clear medieval tradition. The knight seems to have followed Friar Iñigo de Mendoza's verses literally in his lifetime; as he is a Christian he reveres the cross on his rosary but prefers to keep in his coffers the gold offered to him by the demon.

This picture seems not quite typical of Bosch to us; the irony, sarcasm or the sense of humour are lacking which characterize the moralizing or mannerist works of the master of Hertogenbosch, as if he had suddenly forgotten his mocking criticism and was treating the subject with the seriousness typical of those of his works which portray the life

of Christ. Is it that Jeroen van Aken, as all men of his time, is for once distressed by death?

THE SHIP OF FOOLS, Musée du Louvre, Paris.

> «We wandered in search of parts and banks
> And never could find land;
> Our voyages have no end,
> For no-one knows when to disembark
> And thus rest flees us night and day.»

«Das Narrenschiff»
Sebastian Brandt (17).

In 1914, Zafond related this panel to the literary work of Sebastian Brandt, «Das Narrenschiff»-«The Ship of Fools». It seems obvious that the verse quoted from this work in the heading may be a valid basis for Bosch's iconography, but however, the subject is not original and was known in Brabant from the beginning of the 15th century in works such as the poem «De Blauwe Scuut» («The Blue Boat») by Jacob van Oestuoren (18). Its iconological intention is obvious: a satire of society in general and of the clergy in particular (19).

This work is probably one of those with least significance in specific symbols the components of which realistically portray actions forming a generic scene: a Franciscan friar and a nun at a table with a plate of cherries, merrily sing to the sound of the lute she plays. Three other characters accompany them with their voices. Another nun calls out with a mug in her hand which another character fills with a wine cooling in a recipient hanging on the bow. A man crawls towards a chicken, another is being sick, in all certainty sick with drink. Two others, totally intoxicated, are naked and have thrown themselves into the water. Dominating the whole scene a *tarot* figura sits on a branch sipping from a cup of the generous wine which puts life into the whole ship. Here in this figure is the key to the iconological interpretation of the picture. His resemblance to certain characters steeped in folly which illustrate the «Praise of Madness» by Erasmus of Rotterdam edited in 1515 with engravings by Holbein, leads us to identify it with the personification of madness or folly

---

(17) The work was printed in 1494 at Basle, the French translation was to appear in 1497.
(18) This is the theme of a ship transporting a group of parasites.
(19) See the work of Lucien Fèbvre mentioned in note 4.

which has taken hold of all the characters. These latter seemed to be animated by Folly in person just as Erasmus describes it: «Whatever the people around me say (for I do not know how bad a reputation Folly has, even amongst the most foolish), I am however the only one who has virtue enough to distract gods and men. If you want proof of this, think how I have barely come into the midst of this numerous assembly to address you, when on all faces there has suddenly shone a new, extraordinary joy. You have at once unknit your brows and have applauded with frank, merry laughter which, to tell the truth, makes me think that all present here seem drunk on nectar or nepenthe like Homer's gods, whilst a moment ago you were sad and worried, as though you have just come out from Trophonius' cavern» (20).

Bosch's work is prior to the «Praise of Madness», but the spirit and the forms of Erasmus's work already circulated in Brabant two centuries before, their importance growing in the 15th century.

TRIPTYCH OF THE HAY: Sinful Humanity, Prado Museum, Madrid.

> «The world is like a cartload of hay
> and each grabs what he can».

(Flemish proverb) (21)

The two outer doors of the triptych portray a single scene: man on the stormy path of life. How close in intention this is to the lost wanderer in the first canto of the «Divine Comedy»! «Half-way along the path of our life, the straight and narrow way lost, I found myself in a dark forest: it would be hard and difficult to tell what that inhospitable place was like, being intricate and rough... thus my spul, still fugitive, turned round to survey those places» (22). The physical and material state of the pilgrim is deplorable, his wandering through life has left him so defeated that he turns with a rictus of bitterness and melancholy, turning his back on the bandits, on the pair of lechers —the villagers who dance to the sound of the bagpipes— defending himself with a stick against the attacks of a fierce dog. His painful wandering is even further shadowed by the pre-

---

(20) Erasmus of Rotterdam, «Praise of Madness», ed. Madrid, 1970, p. 27.
(21) The proverb is not recorded before 1823, but, as Morales' references show, it was already known in the 16th century.
(22) Dante Alighieri, «The Divine Comedy», ed. Barcelona, 1974, p. 33.

sence of crows which flutter over bones and, above all, by the existence of a gallows, the silhouette of which is outlined against the background cloud effect. Before him a crowd throngs in macabre expectation.

Our personage, although come upon evil times, escapes triumphant from the evils which waylay him. None of the human follies attracts him and those men who do not understand this call him a madman for it is unconceivable for them that he has not let himself be dragged down by passions such as we see in the inner images of the triptych.

The moralizing message is evident, but where do the iconograph and the exagesis of the idea come from? The character has almost always been connected with the twenty-second Major Mystery of the cards (23). He represents the end of the game, in this case life. His iconography in the pack is that of a man with a bundle over his shoulder and a stick in his right hand, and a dog trying to bite him. We do not doubt that the iconograph of the old pilgrim coincides with the 22nd. Mystery but only as far as it defines the image of a madman as it was conceived of in the 15th century. Our madman and the whole iconographic development of the triptych corresponds to the plastic illustration of Psalm XIV (v. XIII):

«1. The fool hath said in his heart. There is no God. They are corrupt, they have done abominable works, there is none that doeth good. 2. The Lord looked down from heaven upon the children of men, to see if there were any that did understand and seek God. 3. They are all gone aside, they are all together become filthy; there is none that doeth good, no, not one. 4. Have all the workers of iniquity no knowledge? Who eat up my people as they eat bread, and call not upon the Lord. 5. There were they in great fear: for God is in the generation of the righteous».

The image of the madman wandering along a path illustrating this Psalm was used by Jacquemart de Hesdin (active from 1380 to 1410-1411) in the «Psalter of the Duke of Berry» (24). In the triptych, the description in images of the whole content of the Psalm is enlarged upon, and one might say, that there one are four basic points in this latter:

---

(23) See J. Combe, «Jérôme Bosch», Paris, 1946.
(24) Paris, French National Library, 13091, fol. 106.

THE HAYCART. Prado Museum, Madrid.

1.º   The foolish man and the evil of his environment.

2.º   The sons of men.

3.º   Yahweh looks down from above on how men have become co-
      rrupted and how not one single man does good.

4.º   Lastly punishment is alluded to, men will quake in fear in due
      course.

We have seen how the first point of the Psalmist's message is perfectly illustrated. When the triptych is opened we see the three acts of the
drama of mankind. The presentation, development and dénouement are
here the creation of Mankind —apparition of evil—, the development of
this latter among men, and their punishment in hell. One may check on
the images how the remaining three points of the Psalm are clearly reflected.

The creation of Mankind on the right-hand door is the only motif not
directly related to the Psalm, but one which the painter introduces to refer to the origin of men —the sons of men— and their original sin. The
iconographic interpretation of this panel from top to botton is: disobedient angels are cast from the Glory of God; like beings representative of
evil, they are monstrous figures, hybrids half-mosquitoes and half-human
beings. De Tolnay has pointed out that this treatment of the iconographic
theme is Bosch's own creation, but the idea of evil identified with the undifferentiated, monstrous beings obviously points to its medieval roots.
After the creation of Eve by the Eternal Father, one of these beings —a
hybrid, part man, part serpent— leads the first human couple to sin; afterwards comes the expulsion and the beginning of human wanderings.

In the central panel, as the Psalmist says, God looks down from above to the sons of men. All have gone astray, all have become corrupted,
not one does good. One might say that this is the apotheosis of human
madness: sin has taken hold of the people and they are moved by sin only.
Bosch uses the Flemish proverb of the haycart which we quote at the
beginning to illustrate in a more popular way the Psalmist's verse. Although Spanish commentators of the 16th century mention it, it was De
Tolnay who pointed out that this panel served as an illustration to said
proverb, but as we may verify this has been no more than a device of the
painter's or the client's to explain the Old Testament principles —it
should be borne in mind that this device is used by the preachers and by

THE PATH OF LIFE. Prado Museum, Madrid.

the master of Hertogenbosch himself to divulge and make Christian doctrine more readily accesible.

The earliest commentators of the picture refer to hay and what it symbolises. Thus Father Sigüenza writes: «... these sons of sin and wrath, forgetful of God's command, which is to atone for their sins and raise their eyes to their Saviour who is to redeem them, to turn each and every one to seek and reach for the glory of the flesh, which is like brief hay, finite, useless, for such are the grifts of sensuality, the states of ambition and fame». All, from the emperor to the Pope, from the nobles to the common people, strive to get a bit of hay, or to attain the *summum* of getting on top of the cart. This latter is drawn by monstrous beings which are clear symbols of the evil which leads Mankind. Father Sigüenza identifies these beings with Pride, Lasciviousness, Avarice, Ambition, Bestiality, Tyranny, Sagacity and Brutality. To my mind, they are perhaps only symbols of evil in the abstract, or in any case the disobedient angels who were metamorphosed into diabolical figures in the previous scene.

On the cart, under the tree of sin, the symbols are the owl —heresy or malice— and the jug —lasciviousness—, the sinners swaying to the music. As usual in Bosch's work, music in an incitation to voluptuousness. A trumpeter demon seems to be playing the infernal dance which leads the sinners on. As a counterpoint to this, there is an angel imploring the Lord on behalf of Mankind.

Yet Mankind will be punished for all this abandon; the Psalmist warns us of this: «They shall quake in fear on that day». Bosch opens up the horros of Hell to our eyes. On the left-hand door, against a highly significant background of a fire, infernal buildings among which the demons and the damned may be seen. The former are easily recognisable because they are monstrous beings with no specific definition in existing earthly forms, following the medieval idea of the malignant being. The damned, naked for they are already dead —here too the medieval iconograph prevails— are accurately identified in the sin for which they have been damned: the lecher by the toad on his genitals (25), or the sacrilegious thief as a jockey on an ox with a chalice in his left hand.

---

(25) In the Hell of the *Seven Deadly Sins,* the symbol figures with proud sinners. Is this a case of symbolic ambivalence? Or is it a mistake on Bosch's part?

TRIPTYCH OF THE GARDEN OF DELIGHTS: Lasciviousness, Prado Museum, Madrid.

«Sy los vieses, jurarias	(«If thou shouldst see them, Thou wouldst swear
que por el dios de Macias	That by the god of Matthias
Venderan mil Jhesus Cristos	They would sell a thousand Jesus Christs)

«Vita Christi»
Iñigo de Mendoza

We are here faced with a work structured in the same way as the *Haycart* and even with a similar development and moralizing intention. In the former, Humanity was criticised as being hounded by the passion of sins in general, whilst in this work there is only one sin: lasciviousness. The master of Hertogenbosch shows himself to be a man of obvious medieval training, at least in his intention in that woman is to blame for sin and is the transmitter of same. Georges Duby writes on the same subject about the Gothic artist that «When certain sculptors and painters decided to portray the flesh of woman in her nakedness, they could not avoid portraying her as guilty» (26). Even in the 16th century, Erasmus wrote in Chapter XVII of the «Praise of Madness»: Woman is an inept and stupid animal; but for the rest pleasing and graceful... What then delights in women is nothing more than folly and thus there can be nobody, whatever he thinks inside, who would not excuse the follies which men say and the silly things he does whenever his appetite for woman is roused» (27).

The closed doors of the triptych show us a moment of the creation of the world. This latter is a crystal sphere, perhaps a symbol of the fragility of the universe as De Tolnay has said. At the top there is a transcription of a Biblical quotation: «Let them praise the name of the Lord: for he commanded, and they were created» (28). At the top, to the left, there is the Creator. The connection between this image of the world with the scenes in the interior is incomprehensible.

When the doors of the triptych are open, we can see the three acts of lecherous Mankind: the introduction to woman in Paradise and, with her, lasciviousness; in the middle, men in the unbridled dance of lecherous

---

(26) Georges Duby, «Fundamentos de un nuevo humanismo, 1280-1440», Barcelona, 1966.
(27) Erasmus of Rotterdam, «Praise of Madness» ed. cit. p. 65 and 67.
(28) Psalm CXLVIII, 5.

madness; in the third act, there is once more a moralizing intention, that which corresponds to the punishment of the lecherous.

The introduction of Adam to Eve by the Creator takes place in a fantastic earthly Paradise —I would almost venture to call it a delivery. The Creator blesses the union. It is here that the evil of Mankind begins. Jeroen van Aken does no more than offer a plastic reproduction of what theologians and poets were writing during the 15th century, following medieval patristics— that is, «Eve's fault». Some authors have tried to see in this panel the iconograph of the creation of Eve, but it is obvious however, that this has taken place and that we are at a more advanced stage, that of the consecration of the couple.

Bosch's fantasy is developed in the description of animals and landscape. Some of these animals have a symbolic meaning *per se,* which comes from medieval bestiaries. It is thought that the basis for the bestiary used by Bosch is to be found in the sermons of Alain de la Roche (1428-1475) (29), but what is impossible today is to find out if all the animals have an emblematic meaning or whether they are simply the fruit of an unbounded decorative imagination. What is not admissable is arbitrary interpretation. Thus a bull, a symbol of passion, is said to be waylaying a unicorn, an emblem of chastity; the interpretation is certainly suggestive, but the animals are not related (to the left of the fountain). Maybe a mocking, merry and playful intentionality has placed a little rabbit next to Eve, for it is a clear allusion to the feminine sex, in these circumstances a truc *leit-motiv* of the work.

In the central panel men allow themselves to be dragged along by their lecherous desires and break into an unbridled general madness, the protagonist of which is sex. The seed, and primal cause of all is Eve, and the Baptist seems to he indicating this for he is pointing at Eve — bottom left corner of the picture—, according to an interpretation of these figures given by Isabel Mateo. Woman, the heiress of Eve, is to lead men to sin and it is highly eloquent that Friar Iñigo de Mendoza should give us all this in three of his verses on the Life of Christ. One should not forget that this work is heavily influenced by Flemish mystic literature. «That

---

(29) Alain de la Roche, a dominican friar, born in Brittany around 1428 and died in Zwolle in 1475. He was basically famous as a man of science, a propagator of the rosary and a preacher, in his sermons in which there is a strange bestiary, the animals of which symbolize sin.

your affections make of your God what you most love is well shown by your passions in whose rhymes and songs passions you call ladies gods; it is well shown by the way you serve them, your continual searching them, your ever wanting to look at them. It is well shown to us by the dear suffering you undergo when you look at them; it is easily shown to us by the dear suffering you undergo when you sigh; your fight for victory well shows memory the faith of your hearts, your holding in high esteem the granting of their wishes; your dancing, feasting, expense, jousting and galas, your singing, letter-writing, working, tempting by night with ladders, your dying night and day to be well-loved by them; if you saw it you would swear that by the God of Matthias they would sell a thousand Jesus Christs» (30). In these verses and in the picture itself, the Ambrosian tradition is taken up, which is also mentioned by Jacob de la Voragine, in the sense that madness came through woman (31).

It seems obvious that in the whole central panel, actions, landscape, flora and fauna are related to lechery. What seems impossible is to be able to justify each of the symbols iconologically within a higler iconological narrative inter-relationship. One could say that, on account of medieval *horror vacui,* there is an addition of fantastico-decorative lascivious actions and symbols, doubtless most of which are of either directly mystic or more often popular origin. The robins and other birds are popular symbols of lechery. In the centre of the panel there is a libidinous parade around a fountain of youth. For Bax, the animals —leopards, panthers, bears, lions, bulls, unicorns, deer, wild boars— are derived from the bestiaries and mystic writings and are symbols of lechery. The mollusc valve which contains a pair of lovers is a normal popular definition of woman according to De Tolnay. For Bax, it is the representation of adultery for he secs the deceived husband in the bearer of the valve. Near to them, an individual in acrobatic posture is masturbating. The red fruit shows that he has reached his climax. In his *Iconology,* Ripa explains that strawberries, raspberries, cherries, madronas and grapes are symbols of lechery. Moreover, one should also point out to the same effect the obscene forms of rocks and vegetables. It would be too lengthy, and in most cases merely subjective —as is demonstrated by the variety of

---

(30) Julio Rodríguez-Puértolas, «Fray Iñigo de Mendoza y sus "Coplas de Vita Christi"», Madrid, 1968, p. 488-489. The work was written in 1467 or 1468.
(31) Jacques de la Voragine, «La légende dorée» ed. Garnier-Flammarion, Paris, 1967, vol. I, p. 264.

THE GARDEN OF DELIGHTS. Prado Museum, Madrid.

interpretations of one single subject— to try and deduce Bosch's intentionality, for it is here that the master's fantasy basically intervenes.

In short, to our mind what is represented here is no more than a critico-moralizing witness of lechery. As we have repeatedly pointed out, Spanish authors of the 16th and 17th centuries also judged him by this same criterion. In the present century, authors such as Xavier de Salas and Ludwing von Baldas (32) hold the same opinion. There are also authors who try to see in this central panel something more than a simple moralizing criticism, and among the different versions we shall give only three, perhaps the most widely kwnown: those of Fraenger, De Tolnay and Sevy.

Fraenger considered Bosch to be a member of the sect of the «Broth ers of the Free Spirit», for which the *Garden* in an illustration of the doctrines of this sect. Sexual liberty was one of the means leading to the salvation of the soul (33). Combe believes that, although Bosch may have known these doctrines, what he really does is condemn them as would seem to be understood from a logical interpretation of the triptych (34).

De Tolnay, taking moralistic meaning as his basis, and attracted by the success of psycho-analysis years ago, offers an interpretation based on the study of dreams. Bosch painted the dream of a humanity desirous of showing the amorous impulses of the subconscious. He uses for erotic symbology the theories of dreams of Macrobius in the comment to the «Dream of Scipio the African» by Cicero (35), as likewise the *keys to dreams* of the end of the 15th century, such as «Les songes de Daniel Prophète» (1482) (36).

M. Cauffreteau-Sévy is the author of a less consistent theory, although an interesting one. The close similarity between the nudes makes

(32) Ludwig von Baldass, «Die Chronologie der Gemälde des Hieronymus Bosch», *Berliner Jahrbuch,* 1917. Xavier de Salas, «El Bosco en la literatura española», Barcelona, 1943.

(33) The last publication by this author corresponds to 1975 (see Bibliography).

(34) Fraenger suggests the opposite interpretation, Hell, Garden, and Paradise.

(35) Macrobius, a writer and grammarian of the 4th to 5th centuries, wrote for the instruction of his son a comment on the «Somnium Escipionis» by Cicero, in two volumes. This is a sort of encyclopaedia of the chief knowledge possessed at that time on physical phenomena. This work considerably influenced medieval erudition.

(36) See in the bibliography the works of De Tolnay of the years 1937 and 1965.

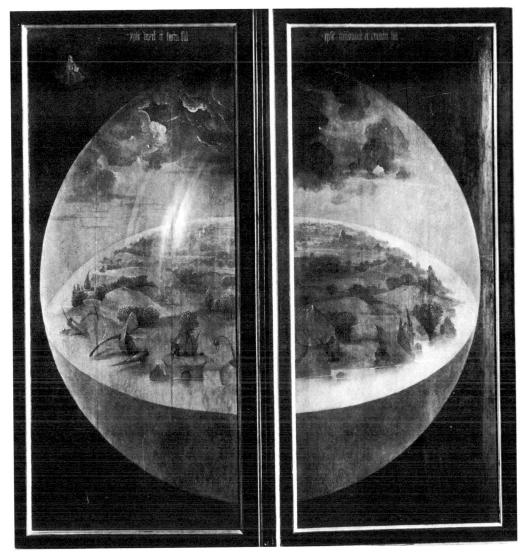

THE CREATION OF THE WORLD. Prado Museum, Madrid.

him believe that they are the same man and the same woman and that each tirelessly repeats unfinished gestures; the men are cowardly and unskillful, the women fearful. It is a parody of love, a satire of the preparation for the act of love (37).

To return to the interpretative thread of the tryptych, we shall now turn to the third act: lecherous Humanity is to be punished. It was necessary to the mentality of the times that this should be so, just as the love of Calisto and Melibea was punished. Punishment is portrayed on the left-hand panel and once more Hell is opened up to our eyes. As against the peace and order of Paradise, the work of the Creator, the confusien and disorder of Satan's realm is opposed in violent contrast (this is the typical antithesis, order-chaos, of the good-evil medieval mentality). This Hell basically coincides with beings or monsters. The damned, according to the medieval conception of the dead, are naked. The towers are on fire. The most important variation is in the motleyness of the scene —the same occurs in the central panel— and in the fact that punishement is only inflicted upon lechers.

In the same way as the fantasy of the master of Hertogenbosch portrays a myriad indecent postures for the interpretation of the *Garden*, the same thing occurs in this diabolic mansion, in which a specific punishment exists for the different types of lechery. We are faced with similar difficulties to those of the central panel in describing each of the iconographic motifs individually. However, the symbols which undeniably refer clearly to lechery are: the glass, lantern, feminine emblems; knives and skates are masculine symbols; in the giant goose, a diabolical tavern with the obscene sign of the bagpipes; the mounting of the staircase symbolizes the sexual act. What most draws one's attention is the punishment undergone with musical instruments. Geuffreteau-Sévy has written: the man impaled on the harp strings is one of the most disconcerting bits of painting in all of Bosch's repertoir». Music in Bosch's work is always there to introduce woman who listens to it in the voluptuousness of carnal sin, and thus we see it in the lechery of *The Seven Deadly Sins* or in the pair of lovers in the *Haycart.* Once more, Jaroen van Aken does no more here than adapt the mystic and moral principles then prevailing in his native Brabant, as these words of Dionysius the Cartusian monk confirm: «But when this artificious mysticism serves to please the

---

(37) M. Gauffreteau-Sévy, «Hieronymus Bosch», el Bosco, 3rd. ed. Madrid, 1973.

ear and serves to please those present, mainly the women, then it should be rejected without any deubt» (38). The musical instruments which had served for carnal delight are now used to torture the sinner.

We should not like to finish this description without a mention of the enigmatic face under the lecherous bagpipes. Some historians consider it to be a self-portrait of the master, thus interpreting Hell as a vision of which he is the dumb witness.

THE MAN: or THE PRODIGAL SON, Boymans-van-Beuningen Museum, Rotterdam.

«I know not who I am nor where I must go»

«Bercheidenheit» by Freidank

The majority of historians think that this picture represents the *prodigal son* (St. Luke, 15: 11-25) (39). We shall never know if this is a self-portrait of Bosch as Hanema says, but what is obvious is that the protagonist symbolises sinful humanity, particularly lechery, who leaves this way of life to choose the path of the Saviour indicated by the woodpecker.

The house is a brothel, the swan and the jug are highly significant emblems of this. In the doorway a couple are coming to an agreement over their carnal deal, the jug carried by the woman seems to point to this. In the corner a man urinates after intercourse and at the window a woman watches our man depart. This latter, rather than a specific individual, is a prototype of a materially and morally ruined man.

The message which the picture seems to convey fully coincides with the evangelical subject of the *prodigal son,* hence the confusion in his identification. However, from the iconographical point of view, there is only one element which coincides with this subject, the sow suckling her

---

(38) Dionysius the Cartusian, «Opera Omnia», vol. XXXVII, p. 197. (Quoted by John Huizinga, «El otoño de la Edad Media», 7th ed. Madrid, 1967.

(39) Recently, Nicolás Calas, on commenting upon the paintings The Prodigal Son and his alter ego The Wanderer of the Triptych of the Hay, tries to show the unreconciliable contradictions between the interpretations of the allegorical meaning of the «Parable of the Prodigal Son» according to St. Augustine and St. Jerome («Hieronymus Bosch, The parable of the two Brothers», *Coloquio,* 37, 1978, P. 24-33).

young. For the rest, if this iconograph corresponds to the theme in question, it would be quite novel. The most important thing in this work, to our mind, is what is what it seems to convey in vital experience. All critics coincide in dating this work in Bosch's mature period. We would say that this maturity is not only of a technical nature but of a human one, too. There is no ironic sarcasm in the work, but melancholy, the melancholy of one who has seen everything and, like a tramp, goes out onto the road bidding farewell to the pleasures of life, which, as the poet says: «when remembered, give sorrow».

We would venture to say that, if this is not a physical portrait, it is in fact a plastic transposition of Bosch's own state of mind. Disdain for the worldly is obvious. A pessimistic interpretation of the work would relate the iconograph to Freidank's verse (40) on disoriented man. However, the presence of the woodpecker, a symbol of the Saviour, seems to indicate choice of the right path which makes for greater optimism for sinful mankind.

OPERA DISJECTA

As an appendix to this catalogue of works with man as protagonist, with all his sins and virtues, we should like to discuss certain works which may be included under this heading, but which, either on account of their state of preservation —fragmentary or with modern repainting— or are known only through literary quotations, will not allow us a closer iconological approach, at least in the work of synthesis.

THE DEATH OF THE JUST MAN, THE DEATH OF THE REPROBATE, Wildenstein Gallery, New York.

These two panels come from a triptych whose central panel is missing and which probably represented the *Last Judgement* (41). The lack of this latter which in all certainty conditioned an iconographic interpretation of the side panels, and the not-absolute confirmation of its authorship have led us to not include it.

---

(40) With the name of «Freindank Bescheidenheit» a collection of rhymed axioms is known which date from the first half of the 12th century and which deal with political and religious questions (see W. Grimm, «Freidanks Bescheindenheit», Gothinga, 1834).

(41) De Tolnay, in the 1965 edition of his book, includes a possible copy of the Ghent original, in which there are too many innovations on Bosch's characterictics for it to be taken into account.

ALLEGORY OF PLEASURES, University Art Gallery, Yale.

A far too fragmentary work, 31 × 35 cms. in which we see themes and types recreated which are characteristic of Bosch's production of a moralizing nature, more specifically in the deadly sins: *lechery* (a pair of lovers in the inside of a tent); *gluttony* represented by a fat man on a floating bucket from which wine flows.

HEAD OF A WOMAN, Boymans-van - Beuningen Museum, Rotterdam.

Its size is so small, 13 × 5 cms., that it is almost impossible to discuss at all. It is not of course an insolated portrait but probably a fragment of a donor in a larger composition (42).

THE TRIPTYCH OF THE FLOOD, Boymans-van - Beuningen Museum, Rotterdam.

In a very bad state of preservation, its authoriship is controversial, neither is the general ordering of the ensemble known. In general terms, its iconological problems revolve around human sin and its correction: *The evil world, the devil at home, the devil in the country, the world after the Flood, the man who is lost through sin, the soul of the blessed.*

VISIONS OF THE HEREAFTER, Ducal Palace, Venice.

The wings of two triptyches whose central panels have been lost. It is supposed that they were the *Last Judgement* and the *Resurrection.* Of a most doubtful ordering. From the fragments preserved, we may clearly appreciate the good-evil antithesis, as likewise that of reward-punishment: *The ascent into Heavan, The fall of the damned, The Earthly Paradise, Hell.*

THE LAST JUDGEMENT, Alte Pinakothek, Munich.

A fragment from the central panel of a triptych whose wings have not been preserved. The resurrection of the flesh is the matter iconographed here.

---

(42) If we except the *Head of the Crossbowman* which the Prado Museum Catalogue alone acknowledges as an original, we know of no isolated portrait painted by him. This is strange, for it is one of the characteristics of Flemish painting, so inclined to portray its chief burgesses.

THE PRODIGAL SON. Museum Boymans-van-Beuningen, Rotterdam.

TRIPTYCH OF THE JUDGEMENT, Groeninge Museum, Bruges.

An over-restored work with excessive inventions and of controversial authorship.

MISSING WORKS

Through literary mentions, we know of the existence of more than 70 of the master of Hertogenbosch which are not currently preserved. We shall discuss here those which might fall within the spirit of this section of the catalogue. They fall under three groups which may better define them, although of course, it is impossible for us to enter into iconological interpretations, but which might help to give us a clearer idea of Bosch's iconography (43).

Human types

The man who repairs bellows and lanterns (44). *The organist's assistant* (45). *A Witch* (46). *A Sorcerer* (47). *The monster-child* (48). *A Sovereign* (49). *Physiognomic studies for a character* (50). We give below several pictures on blindness which would have been of great interest in order to compare them with Peter Breugel (1525-1589)'s types: *The Blind Men* (51) *Three Blind Men* (52); *Blind Men Boar-Hunting* (53).

---

(43) The works quoted below have been taken from the work by Mia Cinotti, «El Bosco», Barcelona, 1968, p. 116-117.

(44) A Painting on a panel which is quoted in 1603 in the inventory of Marco Núñez Pérez's goods.

(45) A figure working the organ bellows, mentioned among the works in the Pardo.

(46) This is a canvas acquired by Philip II which appears in the inventory of the Madrid Royal Palace in 1598.

(47) A Tempera painting quoted in the inventory of the Madrid Royal Palace in 1636.

(48) A strange child born in Germany, «who at the age of three days looked seven... whom its mother wrapped in swaddling clothes», mentioned by Argote in «Discurso sobre el libro de la Montería», Madrid, 1583.

(49) Panel painting, which figures among the belongings of Herman de Neyt in an inventory of 1642.

(50) A canvas inventoried with the belongings of Michiel van der Heyden in 1552.

(51) Tempera on canvas mentioned in the Pardo inventory after the fire of 1608.

(52) A canvas acquired in 1570 by Philip II from the heirs of Guevara. It shows a blindman who guides another and behind them, there is a blind woman. The description reminds one of the *Parable of the Blind* by Peter Bruegel.

(53) A canvas quoted in the inventory of the Royal Palace in 1598, after Philip II's death.

Mannerist Scenes

Nuptial Banquet (54). *Nuptial Pact* (55). *Pastoral* (56). *Flemish Dance* (57). *The Test for Heresy* (58). *Man upon Ice* (59). *Two Pictures on the Cure for Madness* (60). *Bailiffs leading an arrested man* (61).

Sin and its Punishment

The Seven Deadly Sins (62). *The Last Judgement* (63). *Lent and Carnival* (64).

VITA CHRISTI

We saw in the introduction to Bosch's works of social criticism how people's faith in the 15th century had become profanated. The religious vinculation of this faith was supplied by intermediaries, the clergy, who showed themselves to be less and less pure and who took an increasingly large part in their own sins. In the 14th century, certain exceptional spirits had reacted against the corruption of habits among the clergy. Ruysbroeck (1293-1381) (65) wrote against this attitude of the monks: «To the madness which today reigns in the cloisters there is added the

---

(54) This appears among the belongings of Peter Paul Rubens, in an inventory carried out after the painter's death.

(55) This would be a fresco according to the Pardo inventory after the fire of 1608.

(56) Quoted among the belongings of Herman de Neyt in the 1642 inventory.

(57) A canvas acquired by Philip II from Guevara's heirs in 1570. If this is the same as that described by Cean Bermúdez in 1800, it was a picture of a drunken orgy with ridiculous figures.

(58) This was in Jan Dietring's house in 1604. A monk threw the heretical books into the flames together with his own and only this one was saved from the fire.

(59) The figure bore on its head a horse-skull. It was in the Pardo Palace after the fire of 1608.

(60) One was in the palace of Duke Ernst of Austria, according to the 1595 inventory. In it, doctors and surgeons extracting a stone from the patient's head were portrayed. The other picture was tempera on canvas and was mentioned in the 1598 inventory of the Royal Palace.

(61) A canvas inventoried in the Royal Palace in 1607.

(62) This appears in the inventory of the belongings of Margarethe Boge in 1574.

(63) An oil panel, sent to San Lorenzo del Escorial in 1593. It came from the sale of the belongings of Prior Ferdinand, the bastard son of the Duke of Alba and from the same sale came the *Triptych of Delights.*

(64) Mentioned in the Pardo inventories after the fire of 1608. Later it was to be the subject of the battle between Carnival and Lent which was so typical of the literature of the Lower Middle Ages.

(65) From 1343 until his death he lived secluded in the forest of Soignes in the hermitage of Groenendal, which became famous for the works he wrote there.

use of another type of adornment: the silver-plated belts of the type which have several pendants hanging at each side and which tinkle when moved, so that the young novice, when she walks, rattles all this as if she were a goat adorned with bells. As for the monks, they ride armed horses, they carry long swords like knights; but as far as the devil, the world, its passions and evil, impure desires are concerned, they are unarmed: and they are often vanquished» (66). After this criticism, Ruysbroeck, it should not be forgotten that he was a mystic, advocates a closer union with Jesus Christ —«Noces Spirituelles»— to achieve a reform of lax customs.

The choice of this fragment from Ruysbroeck has been specially made for two reasons: firstly, because it sums up in a text of the time the criticism and reaction against a dissolute clergy, proposing a nearer approach to Christ the man; secondly, the whole reformist spirit of the Flemish *devotio moderna* and the rest of the theologians and moralists who converged in the *pure Christianty* of Earasmus of Rotterdam were based on this mystic of the 14th century. The second half of the 15th century is characterized by a wide diffusion of religious tracts in which this reformist spirit of the Church prevails and which springs from its own militants. The printing press contributed notably to this diffusion of texts. Between 1455 and 1520, 75 % of the books printed were religious ones. We said in the previous chapter that this reform could be defined as a return to the sources of Catholic Christianity, as is shown by the widespread diffusion of the Bible and its translation into the European vernacular languages. Between 1465 an 1517, seventeen editions of the «Vulgate» were printed; between 1466 twenty-two translations into German were printed.

The God of the early Middle Ages was separated from Mankind and only the clerical caste could participate of His nearness. When 15th century man lost his faith in the intermediary clergy, in order to maintain his devotion to God and to be even nearer to him, he was offered the image which is that of Christ the man, because Jesus Christ lived and suffered like he did, but not in their passions and sins. He served as a model of perfection and above all, man may be redeemed through Him. The evangelists were no longer sufficient; the life of Christ had to be better known.

---

(66) «Oeuvres de Ruysbroeck l'admirable», Brussels, Vromant, 3 vols. 1917-20, «Sept. clôtures», vol. 1, p. 213-214.

The series of «apocryphals» increased and those already in existence were enlarged with new captions which brought Christ even closer to men. A work such as the «Vita Christi» by Ludwig of Saxony became popular and tens of editions of it were made in almost all the European languages of the time. To illustrate the example which men might take from Jesus Christ a multitude of tracts were written in the manner of spiritual exercises, among which Thomas de Kempis' «Imitation of Christ» is an outstanding example. The first edition of this work was made in 1472 in Ausburg. It had immediate success and there were continual editions in different languages.

Popular devotion was especially directed towards the eucharist. It was supposed to be the continued Epiphany to men. But what image was the Christ of the eucharist to adopt? There seems no doubt about the choice: that of the child on his mother's lap in the Epiphany to the Magi (which is the Epiphany by ontonomasia); and above all, the image of the suffering Christ —the *Man of Sorrow*— who by His sacrifice was to redeem mankind and build the eucharistic essence (67). The so-called *Masses of St. Gregory,* so often portrayed in the art of the end of the later Middle Ages, may be the image illustrated by this devotion, Christ shows himself to Pope Gregory whilst this latter is officiating at Mass; the iconographic form which he takes is normally that of the Man of Sorrow and occasionally, that of the Child in the lap of the Virgin Mary.

In the iconographic analysis we give below of those of Bosch's paintings with Christ as protagonist, we shall see how the master is only concerned with illustrating the devotional spirit which characterised the society of his time, in images.

SUBJECTS AS THE EXPRESS PREFIGURATION OF THE EUCHARIST

Before going any further with this exposition, we should like to explain that the *types* of the Old Testament were prefigurations of the Gospel and the basic tenets of the Church, created by medieval and ancient

---

(67) As J. A. Jungmann wrote: «In the liturgical development of the Mass, the action of the Church was no longer to be seen, as in previous centuries, nor its action of thanks and its offerings, but chiefly and almost exclusively the redeeming work of God». «The Sacrifice of the Mass. Historical-Liturgical Tract», «El sacrificio de la Misa. Tratado histórico-litúrgico», 4th ed. Madrid, 1963, p. 144-45).

THE MASS OF ST. GREGORY *(frag.).* Prado Museum, Madrid.

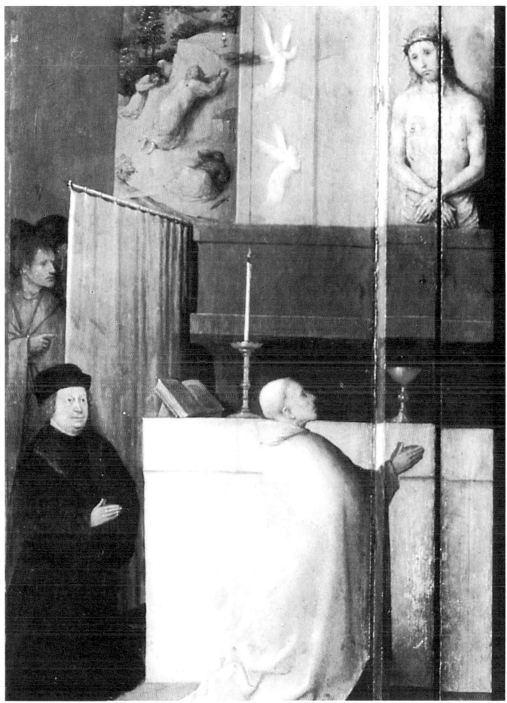

patristics. From the literary image they went on to the plastic image, thus becoming during the Gothic period, the basic of all iconographic pro-grammes (68). These types were introduced in painting and, in this lat-ter, took on certain original forms which are highly suggestive. Types from the past or prefigured ones from the future are painted on grisaille, imitating sculptures which are generally adapted to the environmental ar-chitecture of the scene or to the closed doors of the polytyches. The ba-sic scene of the composition was carried out in its true polychromy.

EPIPHANIES

The *Epiphany of the Magi* had been considered a *type* from earliest times of the passion of Jesus Christ and therefore, of the eucharist. Roma-nesque images show us the Child with the Cross, whilst the Magi adore Him. Flemish painting earlier to and contemporary of Bosch reproduces on grisailles different scenes from the passion around the act of the *epi-phany.* Roger van der Weyden (1400-1464) even shows his archaism when he only places a crucifix above the manger in which the adoration of the Magi takes place (central panel of the *Altar of the Three Wise Kings).*

The literary sources which were in vogue in Jeroen van Aken's time on this subject were: the above-mentioned «Vita Christi» by Ludolf the Cartusian, the work of Johan of Hiildesheim «Dach Buchder heiligen drei Könige» pulished in Strasburg in 1480; «The Golden Legend» by Jacob de Voragine; in 1478 a Dutch version of this latter was published in Gou-da; there ware numerous liturgical dramas which represented this sub-ject (69); apocryphals such as the «Liber de infantia Salvatoris», and as is natural, the Gospel of St. Matthew, verse 2.

EPIPHANY, Museum of Art, Philadelphia.

This work is considered from the technical point of view to be an early one or at least one from Bosch's late youth. To this end the form of the drapery is mentioned, as are the linear ruptures in the bodies, or the pri-mitivism of the composition of the colours —on the basis of vermilion—,

---

(68) It is not that they did not exist in former art, for they can be found right from the earliest Chris-tian artistic manifestations, but that their usage was widespread during the Gothic period, the plastic and the literary-scholastic running parallel to each other.
(69) E. Mâle, «Les Rois Mages et le drame liturgique», *Gazette des Beaux-Arts,* 1910.

pink, gray and black. We agree with this dating but we prefer to take into account the iconography in order to come to the same conclusion. Friedlander sees in the work the influence of Van der Weyden. We are of the opinion that, on account of the environment round the manger, the forms and attitudes of the Magi and above all their dress, this picture is really connected with the tens of *Epiphanies of the Magi* illustrating *hour books, moralized Bibles, Psalters,* etc. of the 14th and 15th centuries.

What is there new about the iconography? Practically nothing. Both space and figures fit in with medieval tradition, even the presence of the persons is right. This gives the work a certain air of iconographic archaism for the time (70). However, there are two small iconographic details, we could almost say iconographic accidents, which reinforce the iconological message with images: the instruments of the offering and the scene from the *fall of manna* on the black king's sleeve (71).

The coffers for the gifts of the Magi are liturgical objects and for De Tolnay they prefigure the Mass. If we look closely we see that they are a chalice, a reliquary —possibly a staurotheque— and an ostensory. The interpretation of these symbolic instruments coincides with that which we shall give to the Prado Epiphany: the Magi announce the Godhead, the sacrifice on the Cross —the staurotheque— and the ostensory or monstrance refers to the eternal presence of Chirst in the host, His epiphany to men (72). This idea is confirmed by the fact that the same Magus has on his sleeve the scene of the manna, a direct allusion to eucharistic bread. St. John put these words in Christ's mouth: «I am the bread of life; your forefathers ate manna in the desert and died. This is the bread which comes from heaven, so that he who eats of it shall not die» (73).

The falling of manna in the desert (Exodus XVI, 14), as De Tolnay has pointed out, is a presage of the *last supper* and he tries to show this by

---

(70) The train of the Magi is enlarged to take on the proportions of a crowd as from the *Altar of the Three Wise Kings* (1440-5) by Stefan Lochner (1405-1451).

(71) The names of the Magi were still not yet defined at this time according to their origin and it is quite normal to see how text and images vary to this effect.

(72) «The history of the mostrance or ostensory, which in the Latin is the word *monstrancia,* began in the first half of the 14th century, that is, when the habit of exposing the host to the eyes of the faithful without humeral veils was introduced», Mario Righetti, «Historia de la Liturgia», 2 vols., Madrid, 1955, vol. I, p. 520.

(73) Gospel according to St. John, VI, 48-50.

quoting examples from the «Biblia pauperum» (74) and the «Speculum humanae Salvationis» (75). However, there is no doubt here that it refers not to its own institution, but to the presence of Christ in the Host as the eucharistic bread, as may be deduced from the reading of the Gospel of St. John.

TRIPTYCH OF THE EPIPHANY, Prado Museum, Madrid.

We have already referred to the plastic quality of the work which is a clear exponent of Bosch's mature period and, curiously, a work complicated iconology.

The doors of the triptych when closed show scenes of the so-called *Mass of St. Gregory* (76). As we shall see below (in the Christologic cycle of the Passion) this is the magnified expression of the Eucharist, just as Pope St. Gregory himself defined it: «Through the mystery of this Host, Jesus suffers a new death for us, for we renew His Passion just as many times as we offer Him the Host of His Passion» (77). This *Epiphany of Christ* as mentioned in the Eucharist, showing us Him as the God-Man, suffering during the Passion in exactly the same manner, is symbolically prefigured on the inside in the *Epiphany of the Magi*.

The two figures of kneeling laymen have been identified by De Tolnay: the one on the left is the dead father of the donor; the one on the right is the Roman woman who doubted the presence of Christ in the Eucharist.

When the wings of the triptych are open the *Epiphany of the Magi* is displayed to view, although over the three panels, the work shows true

---

(74) The «Bibles of the poor» were at first in manuscript form and were concordances between the Old and New Testaments. Their wide diffusion was due to their use of xylographs and the first were written at the beginning of the 15th century in Latin. There were French versions later and, between 1470 and 1490, two editions were made in German.

(75) Also called «speculum salutis». Its origin goes back to the 13th and 14th centuries and matters from the Old and New Testaments are dealt with in it.

(76) We have already discussed its popular meaning in the introduction. As for the iconographic origin, it is imprecise, and at first had an image of the *Christ of the Pieta* in the centre, also called in Biblical terms, *The Man of Sorrow*. This image really came from the East, from Jerusalem and was not introduced until the beginning of the Middle Ages into the West, where it spread rapidly at the begining of the 15th century.
On this matter, see Gertrud Schiller, «Iconography of Christian Art», vol. 2, London, 1972, p. 199 ff.

(77) Sermon 17 of the 2nd book of «Sermons on the Gospels». «Obras de San Gregorio Magno», Madrid, 1958, p. 741 ff.

unity through the background landscape. In the intepretation of the picture we find iconological themes at four levels: Old Testament motifs which
announce the Epiphany, the development of same, Old and New Testament elements which prefigure the Eucharist, and the personification of
the chief burgesses.

The Old Testament motif which presages the Epiphany is represented
in Balthasar's metallic cape, which shows the Queen of Sheba offering
her gifts to Solomon. The Biblical text says: «And she came to Jerusalem
with a very great train, with camels that bare spices, and very much gold,
and precious stones...» (I Kings, X, 2 and 10). The identification of Solomon with Jesus is obvious: the action of offering by a Queen of Sheba
became far more suggestive as a *type* of the Magi when literature began
to state that the Magi came from Sheba (78). The same co-relation «of-
fering-Queen of Sheba» «Adoration of the Magi» may be observed in the
«Biblia pauperum» and, far earlier, in 1181, in the enamelled ambo by Nicholas of Verdun in Klosterneuburg.

Having examined the Old Testament type which announces the scene
to be developed, we shall now concentrate on this latter. It reminds us in
many of its details of the dependence on the miniature illustrations of the
14th and 15th centuries. Among the most significant of these details are
the narrative nature of the landscape in which there is a statue of Mars
—a symbol in the miniature that Christ had been born in a land dominated by the Romans and dedicated to idols (79); a youth pulling at the hal-
ter of a horse on which a monkey rides; peasants in the fields; armies
wandering hither and thither— they are maybe the troops of Herod searching for the Child; the fantastic aspects of Jerusalem or Bethlehem.
The attitude of the Virgin and Child, the Magi and the majority of those
present is quite normal, even the image of St. Joseph. We can see the
old man to the right drying swaddling bands. In this image Bosch is curiously not with the intellectual avant-garde of the Church which tried to
revalue the image of St. Joseph. On this matter Dr. Johan Eck recom-
mended that on Christmas Eve, St. Joseph should either not be repre-

---

(78) Ludolph the Cartusian wrote in the above-mentioned «Vita Christi»: «They opened up their
treasures and offered the Son of God gold, frankinsense and myrrh. That is, each of them offered him these three things according to the customs of the people of Sheba.»
(79) This same idol, when the Holy Family go into Egypt, falls into pieces. This means that the
world of paganism comes to an end with the advent of the Messiah.

sented or at least should be presented in a suitable way and not boiling gruel (80).

We shall turn to the gifts and the coffers which are essential to the understanding of the ensemble. They have been interpreted over the centuries in many different ways, from an intellectual point of view to the most prosaic of meanings (81). Bosch makes use of an older version, for it is that of St. Gregory quoted in the previous note, which was poetized in 15th century literature:

«Says the first Wise King: «I adore, Thee, God and Man, I acknowledge Thy Eternity, I call Thee beginning and end, and for greater certainty, I serve Thy Divinity with this coffer of incense». Later, referring to the second King, the poet writes: «This King mourns the coming death of the Infant, which he pre-figures with a gift.» Then the Virgin «wishes to mourn the death of her Son», but the third King consoles her: «as it is sweet to the palate after the purge of the apple» so will his words be referring to the Child: «he is to arise the eternal universal King» (82).

Bosch's symbols confirm this poetic interpretation. In the above-mentioned metallic cape the sacrifice of Emmanuel is represented (83), thus prefiguring the divinity of the Child; the Magi, like Samson's father, contemplate God. There is another gift on the ground, and as the poet says, it presages death: it is the sacrifice of Isaac (84) thus reflecting the Passion and death of the Lord. The third King is the bearer of the orb from which an eagle flies as a symbol of resurrection with food in its beak —a eucharistic allusion— to revive its chicks portrayed on the first

---

(80) Quoted by Johan Huizinga, «The autumn...», p. 264.
(81) The most widespread of the interpretations was included by St. Gregory in Book I, sermon 10: «real gold, corresponding to a King, incense is used in the sacrifice to God; the bodies of the dead are embalmed with myrrh. In this way, the Magi thus also preach with their mystic gifts to the Child they adore: in the gold, as a King; in the incense, as a God; and in the myrrh, as a mortal.» *Op. cit.* p. 573. The interpretation suggested by St. Bernard, taken up again in the 14th century by Nicholas of Lyre, is far more prosaic: gold to remedy the poverty of the Virgin, incense to disinfect the stable, and myrrh, which was considered to be a vermifuge, for the Child's tummy. (Quoted by L. Réau, «Iconographie de l'art chrétien», vol. II, Paris, 1957, p. 242.
(82) Friar Iñigo de Mendoza, *op. cit.* p. 424-441.
(83) Manoah, Samson's father, sacrificed a kid together with his wife and after this a prodigy ocu-rred: «But the angel of the Lord did no more appear to Manoah and to his wife. Then Manoah knew that he was an angel of the Lord./ And Manoah said unto his wife. We shall surely die, because we have seen God.» *(Judges,* XIII, 21-22.)
(84) Genesis, XXII. The sculptorial group is on toads, which shows thus that sin is vanquished through the sacrifice on the Cross.

THE ADORATION OF THE MAGI *(frag.)*. Prado Museum, Madrid.

King's crown. This is a clear reference to the men who are the subjects of his kingdom.

There is still one controversial character left to be identified and one on whom countles versions have been given. This is a mad leper — shown by the wound on his leg and his bell. Some have identified him with the Antichrist, whilst others see in him the Jewish people represented by Herod.

THE MARRIAGE OF CANAAN

The Marriage of Canaan has always been considered as an *epiphany,* that is as a manifestation of Jesus Christ's divinity. In this sense we find a justification for the fact that its feast is celebrated on the same day as that of the *Epiphany of the Magi.*

The only one of the evangelists who tells of the miracle is St. John and, as is necessary for its iconological interpretation, we herewith reproduce a few paragraphs: «And the third day there was a marriage in Cana of Galilee; and the mother of Jesus was there. And both Jesus was called, and his disciples, to the marriage. And when they wanted wine, the mother of Jesus saith unto him, They have no wine. Jesus saith unto her, Woman what have I to do with thee? mine hour is not yet come... And there were set there six waterpots of stone, after the manner of the purifying of the Jews, containing two or three firkins apiece. Jesus saith unto them, Fill the waterpots with water. And they filled them up to the brim. And he saith unto them. Draw out now, and bear unto the governor of the feast...» (85).

The subject had been portrayed by artists from the very first Christian art right through to the Middle Ages with just the right number of characters: Jesus, Mary, Bride and Bridegroon, Governor of the Feast and Waterpots. The subject became enlarged as from 14th century miniatures which introduced into the iconograph ambiental motifs of the time, that is they moved towards a generic scene. In the 16th century the motif is a mere excuse for portraying a large feast, a good example of which is the well-known *Marriage of Canaan* by Paolo Veronese. As we shall try to explain, Bosch's iconography of the theme is half-way between medieval

---

(85) Gospel according to St. John, II, 1-10.

simplicity and Renaissance ostentation, but always within the purest orthodoxy.

The iconological interpretation of the picture has been highly varied. Among the most interesting versions, we should like to mention the following: Fraenger gives an astrological meaning in relation to the Sons of the Moon and thinks that the picture represents the heretical marriage of Almaegien to a Jewess (86). Then there are different versions about the different elements: heretical aspects of the food, the owl; maleficient interpretations and heterodoxical ones as to the sideboard in the background, the character with the wand —there are those who see him as a traumaturge; the L-shaped table is considered as an allusion to the symbolism of a masonic lodge, etc. But among all these problematical elements there is one which draws the attention most of all: the child with his back to the spectator who offers a cup of wine to the bride and groom.

When we analyse the iconographs of the picture, we realize that the essential ones are: Christ at one side of the table —it is normal not to centre the scene on Jesus and He becomes gradually more relegated to second place; the bride and groom, an essential part of the composition, in the centre accompanied by the Virgin; the decanting of the water into the six waterpots; the presence of the governor of the feast. The rest of the composition is carried out with the aim of bringing the scene close to the reality of the act, in accordance with the way in which a nuptial banquet of the time was held. Any miniature which portrays a banquet, not necessarily that of the *Marriage of Canaan,* contains identical motifs. For example, the highly controversial sideboard in the background with bowls, flasks and diverse utensils which are hard to identify, is normal in any generic scene in contemporary miniature and painting. It is highly enlightening to compare, on account of their similarity, the sideboard in the feast of King Asuer portrayed in the «Miroir de l'humaine Salvation» and other such examples which would be too numerous for the space of the present chapter (87). As far as the character with the wand is con-

---

(86) Jacob of Almaengien was a Jewish convert to Christianity in 1496, who reached a noteworthy position in Hertogenbosch society. Fraenger identifies him with the grand master of the Free Spirit (heretical sect to which the *Triptych of the Delights* refers, according to the same author).

(87) «Le miroir de l'humaine Salvation» is the French version of «Speculum Humanae Salvationis» and corresponds to the 14th century. Condé Museum, Ms. fr. 1363, fol. 43.

cerned, the one near the sideboard, he is no more than the «governor of the feast» mentioned in the Gospel and was normal in 15th century feast, featuring in miniatures and paintings in the same posture near the sideboard with his corresponding wand (88). In the reproductions of the time there are always two types of servants waiting on feasts: those in contact with the kitchen and cellars, and those who wait on the table with rich clothes and bands, usually cupbearers, exactly the same as the character which certain historians believe to be cryptographic. The food carried by the servants is symbolic, but not maleficient; it is purely sensual with the erotic connotations required by a nuptial banquet: popular allusions to male and female sexual organs (boar's and swan's heads). The feast is of such a popular standard that a bagpipe-player is the sole entertainer. Another sensual reference, and one which is no longer popular, is the archer-cupid. Neither can one accept the above-mentioned symbolism of the L-shaped table for this is a plastic device in order to distribute the characters in the scene to better effect and was quite usual in this type of painting, so much so, that is unnecessary to quote examples.

What therefore is its iconological message? The subject has been used to explain three different ecclesiastical concepts: the marriage of Christ to the Church, the six ages of the world and the eucharistic symbol (89). In order to portray the first subject, the bridegroom had to be identified with St. John; to this end, the artist placed around St. John's head a nimbus (90); it is not shown here. To illustrate the six aspects of history or the six ages of man the presence of as many characters related to the waterpots was also neccesary; this is not specified either in the work. However, the huge bowl, doubtless a chalice, the lid of which is on the table, which the cupbearer holds in his hand and towards which the blessing of Christ is directed, draws one's attention. At the beginning we said that the marriage of Canaan was considered to be a figure of the Epiphany because water was turned into wine there; after the blessing in the Eucharist, wine becomes the blood of Jesus Christ. In this picture Jesus as a priest gives his blessing in order to perform the miracle of transubstantiation.

---

(88) It would be too obvious to quote examples, but a sample may be seen in: fol. 54 v. of Delavigne's work «Description of Anne of Brittany», in the James A. Rothschild collection.

(89) Louis Réau, *op. cit.* vol. II, p. 364-65.

(90) This picture has unfortunately undergone a number of alterations: cuts in the top corners; the dogs were added in the 18th century; the heads are far too much re-painted.

THE CHRISTOLOGICAL CYCLE OF THE PASSION

Popular fervour, centred around the figure of Christ, was eager to see Him in scenes of suffering. Thus people felt comforted in their own sorrow when the saw the God-Man suffering like a mortal.

One could say that the Adoration of the Magi and the Marriage of Canaan were softened Eucharistic prefigurations, but what most impressed the ingenuous hearts of the people were images in which blood, wounds, the instruments of the Passion, the dreadful soldiers who lacerated Christ, could be seen. The mentality of the time smacks of a certain sado-masochism when it not only recreates the Passion in plastic images but attempts to materialize it in the most realistic way possible: passional reliques attained tremendous diffusion in the 15th century: the sacred tunic, the sacred rope, the sacred thorns, the shroud, the drops of blood. Along similar experiental lines, the *Via Crucis* reached truly dramatic dimensions by following the mysteries of the Passion (91).

Artists were to find models in these dramatic mises-en-scène for their images, but they could also go directly to the literature of the time. From the 13th century the Franciscans had been specialists in themes from the Passion, both in their writings and in their sermons. In the 13th century an anonymous Franciscan had already written a little work called «Meditations on the life of Jesus Christ» which was to have a great impact on later literature. St. Bonaventure, also a Franciscan, with his «Philomena», was the inspirer of the «Passion Clock» of the 14th century, in which the actions of Christ's Passion were minutely detailed. At the hour of *prima,* Christ is led before Pilate; a the hour of *Tertia,* they shout «Crucify him!»; at the hour of *sixta...* The above-mentioned «Vita Christi» by Ludolph the Cartusian, the «Golden Legend» and the apocryphal «Acts of Pilate» may also be added to this type of work.

Of Bosch's relatively abundant pictorial work on the Passion, only on two occasions does he specifically express the prefiguration of the Eucharist, and these are secondary works for they are carried out on grisaille and are not specific scenes but the whole of the cycle of the Passion.

---

(91) In Germany the mystery of the Passion at Innsbruck was already held in 1391; in Flanders, passion mysteries can be traced as far back as 1398; this is the very well-known «Passion of Arras» in 1415. A passional mystery play by Arnauld Greban (1471) was acted in the 15th century. (See G. Cohen, «Le Théâtre en France au Moyen Age», Paris, 1948).

The rest of his works in all certainty contain the same iconological message, but as they are fragmented works or simply isolated ones in accordance with the donor's needs, any iconographic context is lacking. One may also suppose, however, that his intentions were so evident for the people of his time that they were obvious.

THE CYCLE OF THE PASSION, *ST. JOHN OF PATMOS,* Sraatliche Museen, Berlin-Dahlem.

Behind the image of St. John of Patmos, the scenes from the Passion according to St. John are told in phantasmagorical figures. There is no doubt about this source for there is a clear allusion to the resurrection and revival of Christ in the Eucharist in the centre scene of the pelican feeding its chicks with its own blood (92).

The main scenes are portrayed from left to right in a circular border: The Prayer in the Garden; the Kiss of Judas, the Arrest and Peter cutting off Malchus's ear in one and the same scene; Christ before Pilate; the Flagellation in Pilate's house; the Crowning with thorns in the praetorium; the Way to Calvary; Christ on the Cross between the two thieves and the Virgin Mary with St. John —one more detail which confirms the illustration from the Gospel of St. John (93); the body of Christi is laid in the sepulchre.

The arrangement of the ensemble seems to be the graphic illustration of the famous «Passion Clocks» we mentioned above.

THE CYCLE OF THE PASSION, IN THE *TRIPTYCH OF THE EPIPHANY,* Prado Museum, Madrid.

Although the content of the cycle is more or less the same as the previous one and the meaning identical, they are different in intention: in the former the continued presence of Christ in the Eucharist in which the Passion is renewed. But now, Bosch is illustrating the *Mass of St. Grego-*

---

(92) Here as before in the Prado *Epiphany,* the image of a pelican feeding its chicks is juxtaposed with that of the eagle of the resurrection which is in turn the emblem of St. John. The identification of the pelican as a Redemption and Eucharist symbol already appears in St. Albert, St. Thomas, St. Bernard...

(93) The Gospel according to St. John is the only one which refers to the presence of the saint together with Mary at the foot of the Cross (John, 19, 26).

ST. JOHN AT PATMOS. Staatliche Museen, Berlin-Dahlem.

ry. This image, as we have stated above, was highly successful in the 15th century for it confirmed the Epiphany of Christ in the Host in images.

The passional motifs illustrated are, from top to bottom and right to left, as follows: The Prayer in the Garden, the Arrest, Christ before Pilate, the Flagellation, the Crowning with Thorns, the Way to Calvary —with Veronica— and the Crucifixion on the hill with St. John and the Virgin. This is no longer specifically the Gospel of St. John but a synthesis of the four Gospels, as may be shown by the presence of Veronica or the Virgin and St. John. There are even scenes of great picturesqueness which tell of inspiration in passional apocryphals: the devil carrying the bad thief's cross or the father carrying his child to see Judas hanged. The image of the pelican has been substituted by Christ emerging from the sepulchre.

OTHER SCENES FROM THE PASSION

The Arrest of Christ

In the two former cycles we saw how three different moments of the action were juxtaposed: the Kiss of Judas, the Arrest and the episode with Malchus. As an individual scene it is only repeated on a grisaille of the triptych of the *Temptations* in Lisbon.

The scene now represented occurs shortly after Juda's betrayal. This latter, his mission fulfilled, goes off to one side. In the foreground, «Simon Peter, having a sword drew it, and smote the high priest's servant, and cut off his right ear» (94), «over the brook Cedron» (95), «Then the band and the captain and officers of the Jews took Jesus, and bound him» (96). Except for the figure of Judas, Bosch's realism is absolute, he has traced in images the words from the Gospel of St. John in such details as the presence of the brook, which is not quite usual. In the background, on a promontory, there is the cup of sorrow in the Prayer in the Garden.

---

(94) John, 18, 10.
(95) John, 18, 1.
(96) John, 18, 2.

THE CROWNING OF THORNS. El Escorial Monastery.

The crowning with thorns

The subject is told by three evangelists: Matthew, 27 27-30; Mark, 15, 17-20 and John, 19-2. It was only introduced into the iconography of the Late Middle Ages when the sorrowful image of Christ was of interest. The bailiffs' mocking, irrisory intention was obtained by copying artists of the *feast of fools* in the carnivals, for the evangelical intention is not one of mockery but, according to the interpretation of medieval theologians, torture. Bosch introduces certain elements with an unusual symbology which we shall discuss in the two pictures preserved on this subject.

THE CROWNING OF THORNS in El Escorial.

The circular scene —the circle alluding to the globe— is superimposed on a grisaille in which the Struggle and Fall of the rebel angels is represented. Could it be understood as the vengeance of the rebel angels against the Son of God? Are the soldiers who lacerate Christ the avenging hand of Satan? There is a character to the right of the picture carrying a staff with a glass handle on which Moses is portrayed receiving the Commandments (97). This may perhaps be the personification of *ancient law,* Jewish law, which condemns Christ. One of the soldiers wears a pin with the bicephalus eagle of the Austrians, which is today impossible to interpret.

THE CROWNING OF THORNS, National Gallery, London.

This is from the plastic point of view one of the most mature of the master of Hertogenbosch's works. However, its iconological interpretation is even more enigmatic than ever. What do the turban pierced by an arrow, the half-moon or the spikey collar of nails mean?

Ecce homo

St. John writes of this moment: «Pilate therefore went forth again, and saith unto them, Behold I bring hims forth to you, that ye may know that I find no fault in him... When the chief priests therefore and officers saw him, they cried out saying, Crucify him, crucify him» (98). The iconograph subject which this scene generates was quite unknown before the 15th century and, in the same way as the previous one, artists perhaps took it from carnival scenes or from mysteries on the Passion (99).

---

(97) De Tolnay has identified him with Pilate.
(98) John, 19, 4.
(99) Louis Réau, *op. cit.* vol. 2, p. 460.

ECCE HOMO, Städelsches Kunstinstitut, Frankfurt.

The archaic nature of this work is manifest nor only in its plastic va-
lues, but in the explanatory captions which accompany the iconograph:
«Crucify him», cried the people; «Behold the man» says Pilate; «Save us,
Christ». The image of Christ naked, covered in blood, is no different at all
from similar iconographs of contemporany painters. The same may be
said of the sinister types in the crowd.

ECCE HOMO, Museum of Art, Philadelphia.

This work is compositionally more developed and one in which different acts of Christ's stay in Pilate's house are alluded to: the flagellation,
barely finished —the column and executioners may be seen with their
whips; to the left the reading of the sentence by the judges; Jesus
brought before the people.

In the Art Museum of Princeton, there is a work called *Christ Before
Pilate* which is habitually attributed to Bosch. There is nothing symbolic
in this work, but is has highly accentuated physiognomical studies, the
faces being reduced to bestial masks. One cannot doubt that they must
have left the intended impact of awe on the hearts of the spectators.

The way to calvary

The sources of inspiration are the Gospels (100), although there is a
series of scenes and characters which are included in Bosch's iconography derived from «apocryphals» and medieval dramatic representations. There is not one single iconographic motif, but different scenes are
juxtaposed in the same picture.

THE CLIMB UP CALVARY, Künsthistorisches Museum, Vienna.

The scene is composed of two groups. In the lower one, acting as a
foreground or stage-mouth, the bad thief is portrayed as defiant and quarrel-
some. The Good Thief, makes his confession disconcertedly to a friar.
In the upper part, in a multicoloured, tumultuous group, Jesus weighed
down by the Cross walks on; whilst the Cyrenian, instead of helping,
rests his hand on the Cross. The scene of sorrow and apocryphal motif is

(100) Matthew, 27, 31; Mark 15, 21; Luke, 23, 26; John, 29, 26. There is a fundamental difference
     between the Sypnotics and John: the former quotes Simon of Cyrenia as the one who helped
     Jesus to carry the Cross, whilst John leaves this out.

taken to portray the Child Jesus holding a windmill and in a baby-walker —a clear presage of the *Way to Calvary.*

VERONICA, IN THE *TEMPTATIONS OF SAINT ANTHONY,* Museu Nacional de Arte Antiga, Lisbon.

This is a work on grisaille, which is a *pendant* of the above-mentioned painting of the Arrest of Christ. Its iconography is very similar to the former. A novel elements in it is the fact that the Bad Thief is blindfold, a symbol of moral blindness, for he has just rejected confession. The group made up of Christ and the train has stopped, a moment at which Veronica shows the veil with the face of the Redeemer. A stout character is watching the scene together with his sons. He is the bad example to children so often criticised by the humanist (101).

THE WAY TO CALVARY, the Royal Palace, Madrid.

The scene is more serene here and is more centred on the protagonist, Jesus bearing the Cross, now helped by the Cyrenian. The group of people in the train are separated from the background landscape by the diagonal line of the crossbar of the Cross. There are some blurred figures on this background, Mary and John, and behind them the skyline of Jerusalem.

CHRIST WITH THE CROSS, Musée des Beaux-Arts, Ghent.

This is the last signed work by Bosch. Against a black background, there are only heads around the diagonal axis of the cross. In the geometric centre of the comoposition, Christ raises his eyes in a sweet, serene attitude. To one side, Veronica, her eyes closed, shows the veil with the face of Christ. The Good Thief, anxious and corpse-like, listens to the recriminations of a dreadful Dominican. The rest are horrible human caricatures which shout and gesticulate. At the bottom there is the Bad Thief, with a diabolical expression, facing up to those who insult him. The fact of having painted these dreadful faces to denote the evil they engender is a primitive device although one easily assimilable in the popular imagination.

_____

(101) Brandt in the «Ship of Fools» devotes a chapter to this.

THE WAY TO CALVARY. Royal Palace, Madrid.

THE CRUCIFIXION, Musées Royaux, Brussels.

This is a traditional work in which the painter does not contribute any novelty whatever with regard to contemporary Flemish painting. Christ on the Cross among the group of the Virgin and St. John and that of a donor and St. Peter. In the background, there is an urban landscape — Hertogenbosch.

Literary References to non-preserved pictures of the Passion

Two Crucifixions (102), a Crowning of Thorns (103) and two Ways to Calvary (104).

THE SAINTS

Huizinga describes the value of saintly images in the later Middle Ages thus:»... the saints were such essential figures, they were so present and familiar in everyday religious life that all the most superficial and sensitive religious impulses were linked with them. Whilst the most intimate emotions flowed towards Christ and Mary, a whole hoard of eveyday, naive and frank religious experience was crystallized in the veneration of the saints.» Christ had given us the example, but the simple people of the time felt very far from being able to achieve what the Son of God had done, so that it was easier for them, far more within their scope to attain, to grasp what a man like themselves, dressed like themselves, could do. Their lives, martyrdoms and attributes were known and they were approached to solve all manner of daily problems, for among other things, they suffered the same evils as they cured.

Two sharply defined types should be distinguished in 15th century saints, or at least those venerated during this century: highly popular saints, whose image the imagination of the people had generally disfigured to invent exaggerated prowesses; the other group was far less popular: the message of their lives was more difficult to understand and could be called that of the intellectual elites. A prototype example of the former was St. Christopher, the mythical bearer of Christ, whose image gave

---

(102) A work quoted in an inventory of the palace of the Grand Duke Ernst of Austria (1595); the other was a canvas mentioned by the 1598 inventory of the Madrid Royal Palace.
(103) In the Portuguese church of Santa Maria de Várzea.
(104) One is in Ghent in the church of St. Pharailde; the other is in Bonn Cathedral.

THE WAY TO CALVARY. Museu de Arte Antiga, Lisbon.

people sufficient guarantee against a fatal end each time they looked at it. On the other hand, St. Jerome, a doctor of the Church and Biblical exegete, was closer to theologians and ecclesiastical doctors than to the common people. Jeroen van Aken displays both tendencies in his iconography; as is only natural he was at the service of his clients and even more than this, the final aim of the painting. If we compare certain of the temptations of St. Anthony or the images of any St. Christopher with a St. Jerome or a St. Egidius, we shall see that popular elements and interpretations proliferate in the one and are hardly seen in the others.

Among the literary texts which Bosch may have used to illustrate his works, one might point out the following: «The Golden Legend» by Jacob de la Voragine, the Dutch edition of which was published in Gouda in 1478; a Dutch translation of the «Vitae Patrum» was published in Zwolle in 1490; a year before he died, Erasmus published a biography of St. Jerome.

SAINT ANTHONY

Of the signed works preserved, or those of undeniable authorship —or those referred to in literary texts, thirty-four portray themes of saints. Of these Saint Anthony is the protagonist on twenty-two occasions, without counting the work painted in the workshop. As André Vjastel has put it: «Bosch so enjoyed painting this saint that he has quite rightly been called the painter of St. Anthony» (105). Who was this saint? What meaning had he for the time in which his image was reproduced all over?

He had been the abbot and great spiritual guide of the monasteries of Egypt. From early youth he chose solitude in order to live a life of meditation and in his desert retreat had suffered the most horrible hallucinations. These are explained in a chapter of his life written by St. Athanasius of Alexandria: «He suffered in his person many cruel sufferings, the devils assaulted him with the phantasmagoric forms of wild beasts, such as wolves, lions, dragons, snakes and scorpions». According to the tradition he died at over a hundred in 356. The importance of this saint in the West was to increase as from 1050 onwards, when his remains were transferred from Constantiniple to an abbey in the Dauphinat which took the name of Saint-Antoine-en Viennois. This was to be the origin of the

(105) A Chastel. «La tentation de St. Antoine ou le songe du mélancolique», *Gazette des Beaux-Arts,* 1936, p. 224.

Antonians, a monastic order devoted to curing the sick and specialized in contagious illnesses, particularly the plague. In 1382, Albert of Baviera, the Count of Hainault, Holland and Zeeland founded an order of knights under the invocation of the saint, which from 1420 became limted to a simple pious order.

During the 15th and 16th centuries, devotion to St. Anthony reached its maximum apogee. Almost all over Europe, except for Italy, hospitals and Antonian houses were built; the saint was the patron of different trades: basket-makers, undertakers, swineherds, butchers, potters, harquebusiers... Pilgrimages to his tomb even rivalled those to St. James of Compostelle and St. Nicholas of Bari. But his chief success lay in his healing powers: leprosy, plague and syphilis were the illnesses which, according to the popular mentality of the time, this saint best cured. The effect of these illnesses was like a fire which burnt the skin and for this reason the saint is portrayed on flames, those which he extinguished in the sick.

The motifs which define the saint are as follows: a bearded monk with an Antonian habit, often with a bell, an attribute of all hermits, for with this they defended themselves against demoniac hallucinations; at other times he is accompanied by a pig, but not as a symbol of evil but as his pet; he also usually carries a large rosary and a book with the Antonian rule.

The scenes from his life chosen by Bosch to illustrate his paintings are concerned mainly with three motifs: the demoniac temptation in the terrible forms of wild beasts; the temptation of lechery; and the visions of the saint. All those motifs were widely divulged by the literature in vogue in the 15th century. In the 4th century St. Athanasius had already written a history of the hermit Anthony (106) which was to be the basis of later histories. This biography is reproduced in a chapter of the «Golden Legend» which, as we have said, was published in Dutch in 1478 in Gouda. The same text is also printed in the Dutch translations of the «Vitae Patrum» published in Zwolle in 1490. Numerous legends about St. Anthony became popular in the 15th century thanks to the French translation of a Latin work carried out by Pierre de Lannoy.

---

(106) I was able to read the English translation in R.T. Meyer: *The Life of St. Anthony, by St. Athanasius,* London, 1950.

THE TEMPTATIONS OF ST. ANTHONY, Prado Museum, Madrid.

This is one of the simplest and most tranquil portrayals of the saint. He is sitting on the banks of a stream and seems to be meditating. The monstrous beings mentioned by St. Athanasius throng around him. The pitcher pouring water out may refer to mystic thirst. In general the ensemble is iconographically closely related to the first illustration from the volume «Exercitum super Pater Noster» (1445-50 edition) in which an Antonian is portrayed meditating in the open air, with a hut and chapel similar to those of Bosch's painting.

THE TEMPTATIONS OF ST. ANTHONY, Chrysler Collection, New York.

This work is mutilated both at the top and at the bottom. The eclectic nature of some of the *diablerius* has made some critics doubt its authorship. The saint, sitting reading the book of the «Antonian Rule». He takes up almost all the painting. In the top left-hand corner, there is carnal temptation in the form of a naked woman (see the triptych of the *Temptations...* in Lisbon). There is an allusion to lechery in the mollusc valve closed around one of the figures and carried by another.

THE TEMPTATIONS OF ST. ANTHONY, IN THE *HERMITS' ALTAR-PIECE,* Ducal Palace, Venice.

The same motif as above is portrayed in the *Triptych of the Hermits* on the right wing, that is, lecherous temptation. St. Anthony approaches a pond in a night landscape in which a burning village blazes in the background, in order to get a jug of impure water. He is assaulted by the diabolical creatures around him. The main theme of the temptations is a naked woman in the water, next to the tree with a cloth. This figure has been identified as one of the visions described by St. Athanasius: St. Anthony finds the Devil transformed into a queen bathing near a pond.

THE TRIPTYCH OF THE VISIONS AND TEMPTATIONS OF ST. ANTHONY, Museu de Arte Antiga, Lisbon.

On the closed outer doors, in grisaille we have already discussed the iconography of the «Way to Calvary» in the section referred to.

The open triptych shows the fuller development of St. Anthony's iconography which Jeroen van Aken has painted. It has been given diverse overall intepretations: From the medievalistic vision of the world dominated by Satan and the spiritual battles of the soul to Delevoy's suggestive

THE TEMPTATIONS OF ST. ANTHONY. Prado Museum, Madrid.

hypothesis mentioned above, according to which all these motifs were painted under the influence of hallucinatory drugs. To our mind, Bosch does no more than illustrate with more or less fantastic images the traditional text divulged in the 14th century on the saint.

On the right-hand door, St. Anthony is portrayed being beaten by the devils, and then the saint is led by a servant and two friars. A giant covers some people with his body in order to prevent them from ascending into heaven. The figure reading a letter under the bridge is connected with the central panel and we shall return to him when we describe this latter. All the motifs are included in the «Golden Legend»: the saint, in his ascent into heaven, is beaten by devils; the saint lies as if dead on account of a diabolical attack; when a servant comes to bring him food, he takes him to the monastery; once, the saint awoke and heard cries and singing in the night and, seeing a giant keeping some men on the earth, St. Anthony realized that he was the devil.

The central panel, due to the numerous interpretations given, seems even more confusing than its own iconographic reality. However, there is no doubt that it essentially illustrates the passage from the «Golden Legend»: «One day Anthony was working with his brother and lifted his eyes to heaven and had a pitiful vision; he knelt and prayed to God to avoid the crime about to be committed. When he was questioned of this by his brothers, he replied to them with tears and sobs that an iniquitous crime was about to be committed in the world. I have seen, he said, the altar of the Lord surrounded by a throng of horses which destroyed everything with their hooves: Catholic Faith will be swept away by a horrible torrent and men, like the horses, will profanate sacred things.» Then a voice was heard: «They shall hold my altar in abomination». Two year later, the Arians broke into the Church, split up its unity, sullied the baptistries and churches, burnt the Christians like lambs on the altars. An Egyptian of the Arian sect called Balachius, devastated the Church of God, whipped the virgins and monks naked in public. Anthony wrote to him in these terms: «I see the wrath of God upon thee: stop this persecution of Christians at once for fear that the vengeance of God should reach thee; an early death threatens thee». The infidel read the letter and mocked...» When Anthony was asked by one of his brethren for any way in which to bear the offront to which they were subjected, he replied: «... bear it with patience» (107).

---

(107) Jacob de la Voragine, *op. cit.* vol. I, p. 133-34.

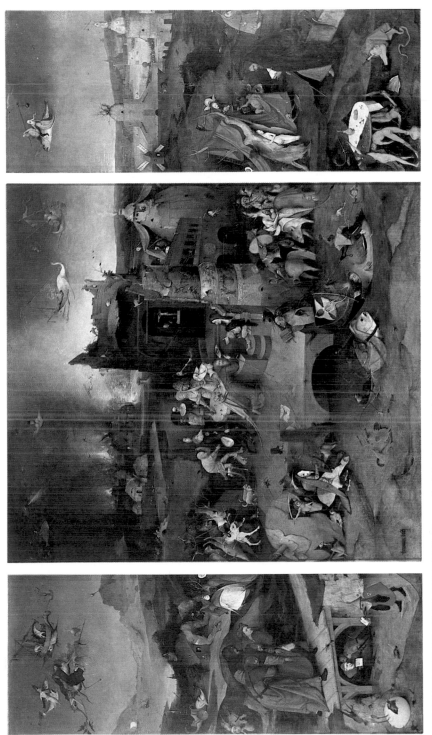

THE TEMPTATIONS OF ST. ANTHONY. Museu de Arte Antiga, Lisbon.

Balachius's army have just crossed the bridge; they have just burnt a church. A large baptistry has been burnt down, the zealous monks have been flung into the water and the heretics amuse themselves. The ruins of a church, in which St. Anthony is, is profaned by diverse acts. A burlesque representation of the Eucharistic banquet, a nun holds out her hand to take the «holy grail»; a devil officiates a mass lower down; there is a figure in the water inside a strange boat mocking the letter he has just read —we believe that this figure, or the one under the bridge, on the right-hand door, may be Balachius reading and mocking St. Anthony's letter. This is in general terms, the interpretation which the master of Hertogenbosch has given to the previous paragraph. He has even juxtaposed the dream told by the saint to his brethren, the advice he gives to them that they must bear, suffer, turn the other cheek as Christ taught us. He bore outrage and even made the sacrifice of the Cross which He now shows to us. That is, there is a clear relationship between St. Anthony and Jesus Christ. The saint points to Christ so that his brethren may learn to suffer, and Christ shows us his message, which is the Cross. Being accustomed to *types,* that is to Old Testament prefigurations, Bosch does not hestitate to resort to them here, too, in order to explain that the madness of heresy of the Arians had precedents: in the cylinder in the form of a tower we can see Moses receiving Divine Law, whilst his people have revolted and profanated God by adoring the golden calf built by Aaron (108); idolatric corruption in Beal-peor (109); below, explorers bringing the cluster of grapes from Eschol (110), which here maybe prefigures the true sacrifice, the Eucharist, as against the impious and idolatric former ones.

On the left-hand door, we again find the subject of lecherous temptation. In 1949, Ya Bax, by turning to the source of the «Vitae patrum», explains the scene as the meeting of the saint with the queen bathing in the river. In the background there is the marvellous city to which she leads the saint. The table in the lower right-hand corner, alludes to the temptation of gluttony. The ensemble is completed with other figures which are nevertheles all emblems of evil: two «grilli», fish, devils, two of which are riding on a flying fish.

To sum up, the triptych is an illustration of the temptations and prophetic dreams of St. Anthony with the message that Christ is the model

(108) Exodus, 32.
(109) Numbers, 25.
(110) Numbers, 13.

THE TEMPTATIONS OF ST. ANTHONY. Prado Museum, Madrid.

211

for suffering, as is portrayed on the outer grisailles. As St. Anthony said to his brethren, Christ taught us that when we suffer we must turn the other cheek and, as is doubly portrayed on the central panel, He gave us this example when He died on the Cross.

The Prado Museum preserves a triptych in which many of the themes portrayed in the Lisbon work are reproduced in an eclectic manner, as likewise those of other works mentioned. On the right-hand door of the *Triptych of St. Librada,* St. Anthony is portrayed meditating against a background of a burning city which is occupied by demons.

SAINT CHRISTOPHER

This saint is considered to be one of the fabulous ones for really very little is known about him historically. It is belived that he was killed by an arrow in the persecution of Decius around the middle of the 3rd. century. As from the 13th century onwards, according to the popularized tradition of the «Golden Legend», the man who had carried Christ on his shoulders (111), must have been a giant and thus St. Christopher is portrayed in images. At the beginning, we discussed popular devotion to this saint in the later Middle Ages.

SAINT CHRISTOPHER, Boymans-van-Beuningen Museum, Rotterdam.

The iconography of this work is faithful to the tradition of engraving and miniatures. The subject is inspired by the popular version divulged by Jacob de la Voragine: St. Christopher, leaving the devil's service and the bear-hunt (symbolized in the landscape background), carries the Infant Christ on his back, leaning on a sprouting shepherd's crook. A hermit guides him with a light (bottom right on the bank). The dwelling of the hermit is a large vase —a symbol of lechery?

A private collection in Madrid has a work entitled *Little St. Christopher* in which the same iconographic subject is portrayed with certain variants: Jesus is portrayed within a crystal ball —the world. The novelty is connected with the «Golden Legend» itself, in which it is said that the Child was as heavy as lead, thus symbolising the weight of the first motif.

SAINT JEROME

This saint was a priest and a doctor of the Church (340-420). He was counsellor to Pope St. Damasus, spent several years in Bethlehem and

---

(111) St. Christopher, in Greek Christophoros, means he who bears Christ.

ST. JOHN AT PATMOS. Lázaro-Galdiano Museum, Madrid.

led a hermit's life, devoting his time to the study of the Bible which he revised and translated at the Pope's request. In the 15th century, he was portrayed by two quite different iconographies: as an ascete, half-naked, meditating on the crucifix, and as a Papel counsellor, wearing a cardenal's purple robes. Bosch, in the works preserved by him, only made use of the first motif.

ST. JEROME AT PRAYER, Musée des Beaux-Arts, Ghent.

The saint is not kneeling, which had so far been traditional, but he is lying down leaning forwards with the crucifix in his arms and his hands joined in ectasy. His attributes are on the ground: the Bible and cardenal's bonnet. Another of his attributes is the lion which, as a token of good, is portrayed in the pose of a domestic animal.

ST. JEROME, *THE HERMITS' ALTAR-PIECE,* Ducal Palace, Venice.

This work is in a very bad state of preservation. The saint is portrayed kneeling among the ruins of a pagan building before a throne which acts as an altar. There is a crucifix on the altar. The saint is not praying but seems to be meditating on two scenes which are displayed on the throne: Judith beheading Holophernes —a symbol of the victory of the soul, or, according to the «Speculum humanae salvationis», a prefiguration of the victory of the Virgin over the Devil; and a Knight riding a unicorn— a symbol of faith and chastity.

OTHER SAINTS

ST. LIBRADA OR ST. JULIA, Ducal Palace, Venice.

This is the central panel of a triptych, the doors of which portray St. Anthony and a scene of an unidentified port.

St. Librada was the daughter of a pagan prince who governed Portugal. In order to escape from a suitor whom her father had prepared for her, the young woman prayed to God that she should grow a beard. In his fury, her father had her crucified. She is usually portrayed bearded or without a beard on a Cross, or else simulating a crucifixion. This legend had arisen in the Netherlands and cult to the saint had attained remarkable proportions in Hertogenbosch.

THE TEMPTATIONS OF ST. ANTHONY. Prado Museum, Madrid

In Bosch's work, the saint is portrayed beardless. According to the legend the young man fainting at her feet is Eusebius, the saint's protector. In accordance with this, the dejection of the five thousand converted by St. Librada is introduced. The saint has recently been identified with St. Julia, see Chapter 2.

ST. JOHN THE BAPTIST IN PATMOS, Staatliche Museem, Berlin-Dahlem.

We have already mentioned this work when we discussed the passional cycle, according to the Gospel of St. John. The saint has interrupted the writing of the «Apocalypse» to observe the inspiration of an angel: the Virgin on the moon with the Child in her lap —a direct apocalyptic allusion. The iconography of the work is quite normal for its time: Dürer, Schonganer, etc. In the lower right-hand corner, there is the eagle, the Evangelist's emblem, and as counterpart, and following the medieval principle of good-evil, a demoniac «grillo».

ST. JOHN THE BAPTIST. Lázaro-Galdiano Museum, Madrid.

This work portrays the saint meditating, not here in the desert as is traditional, but in a paradisiac landscape. Neither was it traditional to dress the saint in a red mantle, but in animal skins. These two motifs are not Bosch's creation but belong to Flemish painting of the time. Their meaning seems to allude to Isaiah as far as the landscape is concerned, and the mantle to the saint's martyrdom. He points to the Lamb with his right hand, thus clearly alluding to his state of herald to the Saviour. The emblematic nature of plants and animals is perhaps true, but today, it is more than problematical to interpret them.

ST. AEGIDIUS, *THE HERMITS' TRIPTYCH,* Ducal Palace, Venice.

This is the third hermit of the triptych for we have already discussed St. Anthony and St. Jerome. St. Aegidius prays in a grotto before a sign on which, following the tradition narrated in the «Golden Legend», an angel wrote the names of those who were to be saved through the saint's intercession. The arrow plunged into his breast is that which was destined by the hunters for the doe who fed the saint and who lies on the ground.

216

GLOSSARY

We give below a series of symbols which appear in Bosch's work. We have not given an exhaustive list but merely an illustrative one which shows the symbological problems of the time. All meanings given here were in vogue in the 15th and 16th centuries.

APPLE: This usually refers to carnal sin and occasionally to women's breasts.

ARROW: Laxitude in customs. A hat crossed by an arrow means sexual intercourse.

BAGPIPES: Habitually considered as a malignant sexual symbol. When pink, it means sexual perversity. It may refer to the tavern or the brothel.

BEAR: A demoniac symbol. In alchemy, it corresponds to the *nigredo* of the first material. As regards lechery, the bear is referred to as a taster of sweet fruits. A general symbol of impurity and at the same time of laziness.

BELFRY: A symbol of the power of the Church.

BOOT: It represents hate.

BUTTERFLY: It means inconstancy.

CAMEL: Humbleness, docility. Popular tradition sees sobriety in it.

CAULDRON: A symbol of the devil.

CHALICE: In a wide sense: the Eucharist. In a specific one, the Passion of Christ.

CHERRY: Brought to Europe by the Crusaders, it was considered a paradisiac fruit and is a symbol of immodesty and sexual appetite.

CIRCLE: A symbol of the universe. Some works adopt this form.

COCK: During the Middle Ages, it was thought to be an allegory of vigilance, resurrection, wrath and lechery. It could also symbolise madness and calumny.

CROW: An alchemical symbol «To whiten the crow» was the preparation of Hermetic Mercury. A traditionally maleficient emblem.

DEER: In Christian tradition, a symbol of Christ. The Physiologist draws a parallel with the soul on recalling Psalm 42: «As the hart panteth after the water brooks, so panteth my soul after thee, O God.» Several deer together may refer to the Apostles. Sometimes, it may have a lecherous meaning.

DOG: Envy. When it attacks people, it may also be understood as death. When together with funeral themes, fidelity.

EAGLE: A symbol of St. John Evangelist. An emblem of the Resurrection of Christ. It is sometimes confused with the myth of the pelican. Old Testament texts allude to malignant symbols «filthy birds».

EGG: This has very wide meaning. In alchemy it corresponds to the crucible. It is an emblem of black magic and the devil.

FIRE: An infernal sign. Related to St. Anthony, it means the illness cured by the saint.

FISH: At the beginning of Christian symbology, it meant Jesus Christ. An emblem of Lent. According to medieval tradition, it had a markedly maleficient sense. A fish with scales is a symbol of impurity, according to Ruysbroeck one of lechery and voluptuousness.

FROG: A symbol of cruelty. An emblem of credulity.

FUNNEL: A demoniac symbol of the male organ. When upside-down, it means deceit or false science.

GREEN: The colour of purifying water and also of the malignant gaze of Satan.

GRILLO: Hybrid or deformed human figures. Of classical origin and doubtless symbols of evil.

HARP: As a musical instrument, it means an inducer to the sexual act. In this sense, it has been connected with the swan.

HARE (or rabbit): Voluptuousness, together with terror of death. An emblem of the female sex in particular, or fertility in general.

HALF-MOON: Represents heresy or paganism. The work of Bosch's in which it does not figure is rare.

HAY: Understood as earthly goods of a fleeting nature, inspired by the Psalms: «As for man, his days are as grass: as a flower of the field, so he flourisheth» (Psalm 103, 15).

HEDGEHOG: Vital force. Heresy.

HOOPOE: The soul which accepts false doctrines. Among its magical properties: protection against the evil eye.

HORN: A symbol of virility. An upside-down horn: an emblem of the female sex.

IBYS: A demoniac symbol. The «Physiologist» states that it was the filthiest of animals. At times, it may refer to memory.

JUG: A symbol of a container, as all those of this type, which corresponds to the female world, more specifically to sex.

KEY: An image of knowledge or sex.

KNIFE: References to the male sex. A short-bladed knife symbolises instinctive impulses.

LAMB: Jesus Christ.

LANTERN: An emblem of the female sex.

LION: A demoniac symbol. An emblem of St. Mark and St. Jerome. Tradition saw Jesus Christ in it for it watches night and day.

LUTE: An instrument for sexual attraction.

MERMAID: An effect of maleficient spells, on occasions it may be the sorceress herself. A lecherous symbol.

MOLLUSC: An allusion to the female sex. A figure carrying a mollusc with someone inside, the deceived husband.

MOUSE: A sexual symbol. According to Ruysbroeck, the falsity of the doctrines rejected by Christianity.

OWL: In Antiquity, it was considered to be the bird of wisdom for it could see clearly in the darkness of heresy.

ORGAN: A symbol, like the lute and the harp, related to sexual attraction.

PALM-TREE: The tree of Good and Evil.

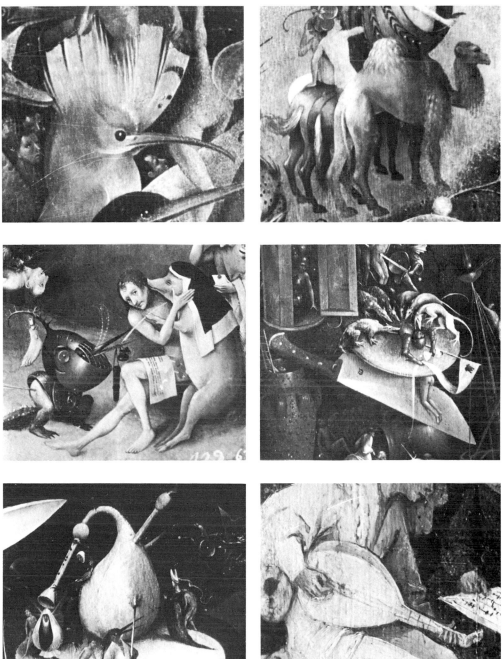

PEACOCK: Vanity. From ancient times, it has symbolized inmortality.

PEARL: Sperm. The human soul.

PELICAN: See EAGLE. An image of Christ. Love to one's neighbours. It fed its young with its own blood.

PENDULUM: An alchemical symbol.

PHOENIX: See EAGLE.

PIG: A symbol of lechery and gluttony. It is a positive symbol when it accompanies St. Anthony.

PITCHER: See JUG.

PUMPKIN: Refers to alchemical crucible, the «concurbit of the wise» cosmic symbolism.

RABBIT: See HARE.

RED/PINK (colour): Love and the Creation.

ROSE (flower): White, a symbol of prayer. In alchemy, the final state of boiling.

ROBIN: A popular symbol of lechery.

SEVERED FOOT: In the language of alchemy, the setting of mercury.

SHE-MONKEY: Inconstancy or lying, occasionally the devil.

SKATE: A phallic symbol.

SNAIL: Universally identified as a lunar symbol. A symbol of the female sex: the valve. The resurrection, for it is an animal found in cemeteries.

SNAKE: Demoniac temptation in general.

STAIR-CASE: To go upstairs means the sexual act.

STRAMBERRY-TREE: According to Father Sigüenza, it means the fleeting nature of earthly pleasures.

STRAWBERRY: Voluptuousness.

STORK: Chastity. According to mystic writings of the *devotio moderna*, it meant worldly appetites.

SWAN: Hypocrisy. According to the mystics, oblivion of the Divine Word. A symbol of gluttony. Its image on certain flags means a brothel. A sexual symbol...

TAU: In cards it means perfection. An emblem of the Antonite or Antonian Order. A symbol of victory over temptation.

THISTLE: The temptations which accost the mind of the lazy.

TOAD: A symbol of the devil or of his spells. A woman bearing a toad in Bosch's work means pride.; in medieval bestiaries, it meant lechery.

TREE: It represents in a wider sense the life of the cosmos. Ruysbroeck sees a symbol of sexual appetite in it. A. Hueco alludes to the crucible of alchemy and to death.

UNICORN: A symbol of chastity. Also of Christ and the Virgin Mary.

VALVE: See MOLLUSC.

VASE: Female sexual emblem.

WATER: Mercy, or hell —frozen water. In alchemy, mercury which a female element is generally together with, water.

WATER-PLANTS: An image of mercy.

WATER-TULIP: Means money.

WHITE: A colour which reflects Divine Power. In alchemy, the second stage of boiling.

WOLF: An alchemical symbol of antinomy.

WOODPECKER: The Saviour, the struggle against heresy.

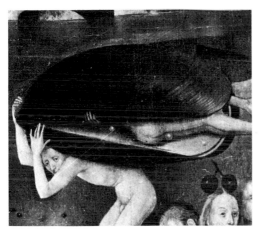

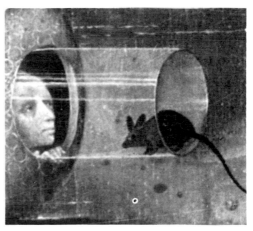

BIBLIOGRAPHY

In view of the countless number of books and article on Bosch, we shall only point out some of the most important as an orientation in chronological order for further study on the subject. Complete bibliography up to 1960 may be found in R. L. Delevoy, *Bosch,* Geneva, 1960; up to 1965 in Charles De Tolnay, *Hieronymus Bosch,* Baden-Baden, 1965; and up to 1972 in R. H. Marijnissen, M. Seidel and others, *Jheronimus Bosch,* Brussels, 1972.

Bibliographical references to texts on Bosch of the 16th and 17th centuries may be found in Chapter I.

1889   Carl Justi. «Die Werke des Hieronymus Bosch in Spanien», in *Jahrbuch der Königlich preussischen Künstsammlungen,* X, 1889, p. 120-44.

1898   H. Dollmayr. «Hieronymus Bosch und die Darstellung der vier letzten Dinge in der niederländischen Malerei des XV, und XVI. Jahrhunderts», in *Jahrbuch der Künsthistorischen Sammlungen des Allerhöchsten Kaiserhauses,* 19, 1898, p. 284-343.

1910   W. Cohen. «Hieronymus Bosch». *Thieme-Becker Künstlerlexikon,* IV, 1910, p. 386 ff.

1914   P. Lafond. *Hieronymus Bosch. Brussels-Paris, 1914.*

1917   L. von Baldass. «Die Chronologie der Gemälde des Hieronymus Bosch» *Jahrbuch der Königlich preussischen Künstsammlungen,* 38, 1917, p. 177-85.

1926:   L. Baldass: «Betrachtungen zum Werke des Hieronymus Bosch». *Jahrbuch des künsthistorischen Sammlungen in Wien,* 1, 1926, p. 103-22.

1927:   M. J. Friedländer. *Die altniederländische Malerei,* V *Geertgen van Haarlem und Hieronymus Bosch,* Berlin, 1927.

1937:   Charles De Tolnay: *Hyeronymus Bosch,* Basle, 1937.

1939:   D. Roogen: «J. Bosch: Literatur en Folklore». *Gentsche Bijdragen tot de Kunstgeschiedenis,* 6, 1939/40. p. 139-46.

1941:   M. J. Friedländer. *Hieronymus Bosch.* The Hague, 1941.

1943:   L. von Baldass. *Hieronymus Bosch,* Vienna, 1943.
        Wilhelm Fraenger: «Andacht zum Kinde. Auslegung eines Bildes von Hieronymus Bosch». *Die neue Rundschau,* 54, 1943. pp. 221-6.

1944   Dirk Bax: «Jeroen Bosch Keisnijding». *Historia,* 10, 1944, p. 121-4.

1945   G. de Tervarent. «The Origin of one of Jerome Bosch's pictures». *Message,* 1945 (January), p. 44 ff.

1946   J. Combe: *Jérôme Bosch,* Paris, 1946.

1947   W. Fraenger: *Hieronymus Bosch: das Tausendjährige Reich,* Coburg, 1947 (English ed. London, 1952; French ed. Paris, 1966, new German ed. Amsterdam, 1969).

J. Mosmans. *Jheronimus Anthoniszoon van Aken alias Hieronymus Bosch,* Hertogenbosch, 1947.

1948   D. Bax: *Ontcijfering van Jeroen Bosch,* The Hague, 1948.

J. V. L. Brans: *Hieronymus Bosch (El Bosco).* Barcelona, 1948.

M. J. M. Ebeling: «Jheronimus van Aken» *Miscellanea Gessleriana,* Antwerp, 1948, p. 444-57.

W. Fraenger. «Johannes der Täufer, eine Meditationstafel des Freien Geistes». *Zeitschrift für Künst,* 2, 1948, p. 163-75.

1949   G. van Camp. «Considérations sur le paysage chez Jérôme Bosch». *Miscellanea Leo van Puyvelde,* 1949, p. 65-73.

W. Fraenger: «Johannes auf Patmos, eine Umwendetafel für den Meditationsgebrauch». Zeitschrift für Religions— und Geistesgeschichte, 2, 1949/50, p. 327-45.

1950   W. Fraenger: *Die Hochzeit zu Kana. Ein Dokument semitischer Gnosis bei Hieronymus Bosch,* Berlin, 1950.

A. Pigler. «Astrology and Jerome Bosch» *Burlington Magazine,* 1950, pp. 132-6.

1951   W. Fraenger, see 1975.

1953   L. Brand Philip: «The Prado *Epiphany* by Jerome Bosch». *Art Bulletin,* 35, 1953, p. 267-93.

G. Dorfles. *Bosch.* Milan, 1953.

1954   G. van Camp: «Autonomie de Jérôme Bosch et récentes interprétations de ses oeuvres». *Bulletin des Musées Royaux des Beaux-Arts,* 3, 1954, p. 131-48.

1955   J. V. L. Brans: «Los eremitanos de Jerónimo Bosco: San Juan Bautista en el desierto». *Goya,* 1955, p. 196-201.

1956   D. Bax: «Beschrijving en poging tot verklaring van Het Tuin der Onkuisheid-drieluik van Jeroen Bosch, gevogd door kritiek op Fraenger». *Verhandelingen d. K. Nederlanse Academie van Wetenschappen,* Amsterdam, 63, 2, 1956, p. 1-208.

L. Brand Philip: *Hieronymus Bosch,* New York, 1956.

1957   O. Benesch. «Hieronymus Bosch and the Thinking of the Late Middle Ages». *Konsthistorisk tidskrift,* 26, 1957, p. 21-42, and p. 103-27.

Ch. D. Cuttler. «The Lisbon *Temptation of St. Anthony* by Jerome Bosch». *Art Bulletin,* 39, 1957, p. 109-26, and «Witchcraft in a Work by Bosch». *Art Quarterly,* 20, 1957, p. 129-40.

W. Fraenger: see 1975.

C. A. Wertheim Aymès: *Hieronymus Bosch, eine Einführung in seine geheime symbolik,* Amsterdam, 1957.

1959   R. von Holten. «Hieronymus Bosch und die Vision des Tondalus». *Konsthistorisk tidskrift,* 28, 1959, p. 99-109.

C. Linfert. *Hieronymus Bosch, the Painting;* London, 1959.

1960   R. L. Delevoy: *Bosch,* Geneva, 1960.

1961   H. Lenneberg. «Bosch's Garden of Earthly Delights, some musical considerations», *Gazette des Beaux-Arts,* 53, 1961, p. 135-44.

C. Pemán. «Sobre la interpretación del viandante al reverso del *Carro del Heno* de El Bosco». *Archivo Español de Arte,* 34, 1961, p. 125-39.

J. Rosenberg. «On the Meaning of a Bosch Drawing». De artibus opuscula, XL (Essays in Honor of Erwin Panofsky). New York, 1961, p. 422-6.

1963   W. Fraenger: see 1975.

Isabel Mateo: «El grupo de la cueva en el panel central del *Jardín de las Delicias».* *A. E. A.,* 36, 1963, p. 253-57 and «El grupo de los jugadores en el *Jardín de las Delicias, A. E. A.* 32/3, 1959/60, p. 253-56 and p. 427-30.

1965   Isabel Mateo: *El Bosco en España,* Madrid, 1965.

Ch. De Tolnay: *Hieronymus Bosch,* Baden-Baden, 1965.

1966   M. Cinotti: *L'Opera completa di Bosch,* Milan, 1966.

M. Praz: «The Canticles of Hieronymus Bosch», in *The Grand Eccentrics,* Art News Annual, 32, New York, 1966, p. 54-69.

1967   D. Bax: P. Gerlach, L. Pirenne and others: *Bijdragen bij gelegenheid van de herdenkingstentoonstelling te's-Hertogenbosch,* 1967.

M. Bussagli. *Bosch,* London, 1967.

P. Gerlach: «Studies over Jeronimus van Aken (alias Bosch).» *Spiegel der Historie,* 1967, p. 587-98 and p. 623-70.

M. J. Friedländler and others: *Katalog der Boschausstellung in Hertogenbosch,* 1967.

E. M. Gombrich: «The Earliest Description of Bosch's *Garden of Delights».* *Journal of the Warburg and Courtauld Institutes,* 30, 1967, p. 403-6.

Isabel Mateo: «El *Jardín de las Delicias.* A propósito de una copia temprana y un tapiz». *A. E. A.,* 40, 1967, p. 47-54.

H. Read: «Hieronymus Bosch: Symbolic Integration» in *Art and Alienation, the Role of the Artist in Society,* London, 1967, p. 77-86.

1968   P. Gerlach: «Les sources pour l'étude de la vie de Jérôme Bosch». *Gazette des Beaux-Arts,* 1968, p. 109-16.

J. van Lennep: «A propos de Jérôme Bosch: polémique, tarot et sang-dragon». *Gazette des Beaux-Arts,* 1968, p. 189 ff.

R. L. McGrath: «Satan and Bosch. The *Visio Tundali* and the Monastic Vices». *Gazette des Beaux-Arts,* 1968, p. 45-50.

1969   E. Calas:«D for Deus and Diabolus. The iconography of Hieronymus Bosch». *The Journal of Aesthetics and Art Criticism,* 27, 1969, p. 445-54.

Ch. D. Cuttler: «Bosch and the *Narrenschiff:* A Problem in Relationships». *Art Bulletin,* 51, 1969, p. 272-6.

E. H. Gombrich: «The Evidence of Images» in *Interpretation, Theory and Practice* (ed. by Charles Singleton). Baltimore, 1969, p. 35-104; and «Bosch's *Garden of Delights:* a Progress Report». Journal of the Warburg *and Courtauld Institutes,* 32, 1969, p. 162-70.

P. Reuterwärd: «What colour is Divine Light?». *Art News Annual,* 35, 1969, p. 108-27.

1970   E. Calas: «Bosch's *Garden of Delights:* A Theological Rebus». *Art News.* 1970, p. 184-99.

H. Heidenreich: «Hieronymus Bosch in some literary Context». *Journal of the Warburg and Courtauld Institutes,* 1970, p. 171-99.

P. Reuterswärd: *Hieronymus Bosch.* Uppsala, 1970.

1972   R. H. Marijnissen, M. Seidel and others. *Jheronimus Bosch,* Brussels, 1972.
1973   W. S. Gibson: *Hieronymus Bosch,* New York, 1973.
1975   W. Fraenger: *Hieronymus Bosch,* Dresden, 1975.
        L. J. Slatkes: «Hieronymus Bosch and Italy». *Art Bulletin,* 1975, p. 335-45.
1976   P. Glum: «Divine Judgement in Bosch's *Garden of Earthly Delights».* *Art Bulletin,* 1976, p. 45-54.
1977   S. Orienti and R. de Selier. *Hieronymus Bosch,* Paris, 1977.
1978   J. Chailey. *Jérôme Bosch et ses symboles. Essai de décryptage,* Brussels, 1978.
1979   D. Bax: *Hieronymus Bosch, his picture-writing deciphered,* Rotterdam, 1979.

INDEX OF PLATES

THE LAST JUDGEMENT. Akademie der Bildenden Künste, Vienna (Pages **57**, **61**).
Closed Triptych: SAINT JAMES AND SAINT BAVON (Page 83).

THE MAN OR THE PRODIGAL SON. Museum Boymans-van-Beuningen, Rotterdam (Page 173).

THE MARRIAGE OF CANAAN. Museum Boymans-van-Beuningen, Rotterdam (Page **189**).

SAINT JOHN AT PATMOS. Lázaro-Galdiano Museum, Madrid (Pages **145**, **213**).

SAINT JOHN AT PATMOS. Staatliche Museen, Berlin-Dahlem (Page 195).

SHIP OF FOOLS. The Louvre Museum, Paris (Page **105**).

THE TABLE OF THE SEVEN DEADLY SINS. Prado Museum, Madrid (Pages **25**, 27, **41**, **89**, 123, 139, **149**, 151).

THE TEMPTATIONS OF SAINT ANTHONY (Cat. no. 2049). Prado Museum, Madrid (Page 207).

THE TEMPTATIONS OF SAINT ANTHONY (Cat. no. 2913). Prado Museum, Madrid (Page 215).

THE TEMPTATIONS OF SAINT ANTHONY (Triptych, Cat. no. 3085). Prado Museum, Madrid (Pages 67, 211).

THE TEMPTATIONS OF SAINT ANTHONY. Museum de Arte Antiga, Lisbon (Page **209**).
Closed Triptych: THE WAY TO CALVARY (Page 203).

TUNDALUS' VISION. Lázaro-Galdiano Museum, Madrid (Page **65**).

THE WAY TO CALVARY. Royal Palace, Madrid (Pages 95, **101**, **201**).

* The numbers in **heavy type** are colour plates.

DETAILS OF PHOTOGRAPHS

Akademie der Bildenden Künste, Vienna, 83 / A. C. L., Brussels, 111, 127 / The Art Museum, Princeton, 103 / E. Dominguez, Madrid, Cover, 17, 19, 21, 25, 27, 29, 33, 35, 39, 41, 49, 63, 65, 67, 75, 77, 81, 89, 91, 97, 109, 117, 123, 125, 137, 139, 143, 145, 149, 151, 157, 159, 161, 165, 167, 169, 177, 179, 181, 185, 187, 207, 211, 213, 215, 221, 223 / Estudio Mario Novais, Lisbon, 209 / Cramer Gallery, The Hague, 119 / Jorg P. Anders, Berlin, 195 / Francisco Marques, Lisbon, 203 / Musées Nationaux, Paris, 105 / Museum Boymans-van-Beuningen, Rotterdam, 189 / National Gallery, London, 53, 193 / National Gallery of Art, Col. Kress, Washington, 113, 153 / Patrimonio Nacional, Madrid, 95, 101, 129, 197, 201 / Photo Meyer, KG, Vienna, 57, 61 / Ursula Edelmann, Frankfurt, 55, 87.